Shakespeare for Snowflakes

On Slapstick and Sympathy

Shakespeare for Snowflakes

On Slapstick and Sympathy

Ian Burrows

Winchester, UK
Washington, USA

JOHN HUNT PUBLISHING

First published by Zero Books, 2020
Zero Books is an imprint of John Hunt Publishing Ltd., No. 3 East St., Alresford,
Hampshire SO24 9EE, UK
office@jhpbooks.com
www.johnhuntpublishing.com
www.zero-books.net

For distributor details and how to order please visit the 'Ordering' section on our website.

Text copyright: Ian Burrows 2019

ISBN: 978 1 78904 161 3
978 1 78904 162 0 (ebook)
Library of Congress Control Number: 2019949611

A CIP catalogue record for this book is available from the British Library.

Design: Stuart Davies

UK: Printed and bound by CPI Group (UK) Ltd, Croydon, CR0 4YY
US: Printed and bound by Thomson-Shore, 7300 West Joy Road, Dexter, MI 48130

We operate a distinctive and ethical publishing philosophy in
all areas of our business, from our global network of authors to
production and worldwide distribution.

Contents

Acknowledgements

To begin at the end: thank you to all those at Zero Books and John Hunt Publishing who have been involved in making *Shakespeare for Snowflakes*.

I'm very grateful indeed to all of the friends who have read over the chapters that follow. All are brilliant and thoughtful people, and I thank them very much for their suggestions and advice, and for making this book better than it was. All have found different ways of gently pointing out when I sounded most pompous, and if I sound pompous in these acknowledgements it's because none of them read this bit before I submitted it: apologies. Many thanks to Lesel Dawson and to Eugene Giddens; to Jan Parker and to Fred Parker; and of course to all the members of 'writing club': Emily Baker, Scott Annett, Lucy Foster, Elizabeth Rawlinson-Mills and Emily Kate Price.

Following the media coverage of the warnings which accompanied my Tragedy lectures, I was very glad of the chance to talk to some of the students who attended the lectures and who had read the coverage. I'm very grateful for their responses (which were markedly considered, mature and intelligent). I'm also enormously grateful to several other students who shared their experiences of trauma with me; their sensitivity and strength seemed to me eloquent, inarguable proof that the blanket term 'snowflake' is not only inhumane but outright stupid. To those students who have experienced trauma and whom I've presumed to talk about in hypothetical terms (whom I've talked *for* and *about* rather than *to*), I apologise.

The piece I wrote for the *Guardian* in response to the initial media coverage of the warnings was improved a great deal after discussions with several parties. In particular I'd like to thank the Clare College English class of 2018: Tom, Cecily, Lizzie, Francesca, Ellie, Anna, Shona and Bea. I'm also very grateful to Peter de Bolla for very kindly reading over the same draft and for taking the time to offer many important suggestions and questions. David Shariatmadari, Toby Moses and Sonia Sodha at the *Guardian* were all involved in the editing and publication of the article: my thanks to them for their help.

Finally, I'd like to thank my family: particularly my mum, my dad and my brother. They will certainly make fun of me for sounding pompous when I say that they all prize laughter and kindness highly: all three of them are experts on both. This was also true of Grandad, who was the person who introduced me to Tommy Cooper (and Morecambe and Wise, and Laurel and Hardy, and many more). This book is dedicated to him.

Prologue

The last time I fainted was at the optician's. I had fainted fairly often throughout my high school years: after my vaccinations against measles and tuberculosis, once while dissecting a pig's eye in GCSE Biology, and, on another occasion — to general and enduring merriment — in the middle of a sex education talk, switching off for a spell as a teacher unwrapped a condom and offered it around for inspection. When I went for my eye test it had been some years since I'd fainted; I was now in my twenties. Nevertheless, sat then in the shiny faux-leather chair, squinting at the serried rows of letters from behind a contraption full of lenses, the old familiar feelings arose: I was going to faint, which was going to be very embarrassing, and I couldn't get out of where I was before this happened. Perhaps I had time to apologise — the tried and true 'I'm very sorry, I feel a bit funny' — but all I knew next was that I'd slipped straight down the faux-leather chair, that the optician, now straddling me, had flung herself bodily on top of me to stop me hitting the floor, and that she was now holding my body onto the chair with a combination of her own weight and a panicked forearm across my throat. 'I'm not trying to choke you,' she told me (reassuringly) as I came round.

I've never yet worked out how much this sort of fainting was *brought about* by a fear of making a fool of myself and how much that particular fear was merely a compounding, accelerating factor. Certainly I've come to recognise that in all of the instances noted here (and the many others I haven't told you about), I became significantly aware of — and troubled by — the fact that I couldn't get out of the situation I was in. Nowadays, in a job which requires me to lecture to large numbers of students at a time, I'm frequently in just such an inescapable situation. I'm more accustomed to lecturing than I used to be, though before each lecture I still tend to get nervous. And still sometimes in

3

the middle of giving a lecture — if I'm familiar enough with my notes that my mind wanders a little — I'll find myself thinking about the situation I'm in, and I wonder: if I fainted, what would happen? In crumpling to the floor unexpectedly I would give the viewer very few suggestions as to how that action might be read. How many of those watching would worry? How many of them would laugh? And if I was sat with them, watching the same thing, how would I interpret such a spectacle?

I leave the Specsavers on Fitzroy Street and walk home; later that day, I tell my friends about the episode in the optician's office and we all laugh about it. I'm still embarrassed — by my loss of self-control, I suppose — but of course in physical terms I'm absolutely fine, and by turning events into an anecdote I feel a little better about myself. No harm done; all in all, I think, it makes for a funny story. It's only much later that I think back over the events immediately after I'd regained consciousness: how the optician had said she didn't feel comfortable continuing with the eye test, how she'd looked shaken, and how we'd had to reschedule. I don't know how long I'd been unconscious, but I was safe in the knowledge that my wellbeing hadn't been in doubt at any point. It was only now, many hours later, that it occurred to me to wonder what *she* felt about the whole episode. In the moment at which I lost consciousness, and in the moments following — holding me up, unable to leave the room — how did she read the insensible body confronting her? And how might that confrontation have affected her?

Chapter 1

Snowflakes

On 15 April 1984, the comedian Tommy Cooper sunk to the floor during the recording of the popular LWT show *Live From Her Majesty's*. He was centre-stage at Her Majesty's Theatre, just in front of the curtain, and was halfway through a skit involving a 'magic cloak'; a younger comedian, Jimmy Tarbuck, was tasked with passing objects from behind the curtain and between Cooper's legs. The audience laughed as each object 'magically' appeared, each bigger than the last: a paint pot, a plank of wood and, eventually, if things had turned out as planned, a step-ladder. But instead, as Tarbuck puts it, Cooper 'dropped on to his haunches and was just sort of sitting there upright with his knees underneath him'. Many of the audience laughed; the performers, too, laughed along: 'we all thought he'd just stuck another physical gag into his set', Tarbuck says.[1] Among the many onlookers familiar with and amused by Cooper's shambolic, clumsy brand of physical comedy, there were some who didn't laugh as his 6 foot 4 frame toppled backwards, as the stage curtains were pulled across him, 'his size-13 boots protruding' and visible in front of the curtain, and as his feet began to twitch. 'I never found Tommy Cooper amusing,' one LWT employee told John Fleming in 2012; 'I never "got" his act — so I wasn't laughing and, perhaps because of that, as soon as I saw him collapse, I thought he was ill.'[2] While several other performers took their turn on stage, an ambulance was called; Cooper, who had suffered a heart attack, was dead by the time the ambulance arrived at Westminster Hospital, some 20 minutes' drive away.

Tommy Cooper made a career out of clumsiness. 'Some comedians', David Quantick wrote in the *Telegraph* in 2014, 'are born funny: we say they have funny bones, as though their sheer comedicness infuses their entire body and soul. And one such comedian was the late Tommy Cooper.'[3] Many of Cooper's fans find the phrase useful: the actor David Threlfall arguing, for instance, that 'his bones were funny, that's just the way he was'; Jimmy Tarbuck, reflecting on Cooper's death, said too that 'Tom had funny bones.'[4] The comedian Tim Vine believes Cooper 'was physically hilarious with the way he looked and held himself', adding, 'I mean, when you can breathe out and it's funny, who needs material?'[5] Given how central Cooper's physicality was to his on-stage persona, it's understandable that many of those present interpreted his heart attack as 'another physical gag'. Search through the accounts of Tommy Cooper's death, though, and it's clear that there wasn't a consensus interpretation of his fall to the floor at the time: while some people laughed, others did not; while other acts were performed obliviously in front of the curtain, desperate efforts were made to resuscitate Cooper a few feet behind it; the audience in the theatre were unaware of Cooper's condition, by and large, but LWT abruptly stopped broadcasting the show before cutting quickly to adverts. In short, nobody knew whether Cooper was *ok*.

While different onlookers might always have different reactions to the same spectacle, the kinds of actions which we might term slapstick seem to elicit a particularly volatile range of responses. As I'll show in the chapters to come, when bodies are presented as inscrutable, inexplicable and out of control, they can be found amusingly *or* distressingly alien. In the examples I've given here, the slapstick action doesn't seem to have any *a priori* comic or traumatic quality inherent to it. The footage of Cooper at Her Majesty's Theatre hasn't been broadcast on any television networks since he died, but it has been uploaded to Youtube on several occasions (something noted by media reports in 2009 and 2014; and, at time of writing, the footage has since been uploaded to Youtube by users in 2016 and twice in 2018). Scroll through the comments below these videos and you'll find people bickering about whether or not the action of Cooper falling down was funny or not. One user, 'TreyAllDay', is adamant that 'that shit wasnt even funny he just sat down and laid down', which arouses the disagreement of several other users; 2 months after TreyAllDay's initial comment, for instance, another user, 'ThatGuyYouArent2', cites a number of other successful comic performers in taking issue with TreyAllDay's analysis:

> Yeah, and Robin Williams just did some stupid voices. David Mitchell just complains about things that annoy him. George Carlin told everyone they were stupid.
> Pretty much any comedy can be made unfunny if you describe it literally. This was what the dude was known for – the comedy came from his delivery, not the actual content.

Perhaps TreyAllDay is right to be criticised — for not attending more to Cooper's 'delivery', or not being more aware of context (as another user puts it, 'it was funny back then cause tommy cooper did shit like that all the time').[6] But his retort — 'Bruh in what universe is laying down funny'? — does highlight how challenging and how ambiguous this unexplained physical action is when considered in isolation.

Another user, 'Lickopotamus Slurperton', muses that the footage proves 'that "comedy" and "tragedy" aren't all that different sometimes'. When considering the Youtube comments *en masse*, it becomes clear these labels rarely arise as an individual's affective response to the spectacle of Cooper's fall in isolation. Many of those comments talk about Cooper's fall in relation to the gaze of the audience members who were present, and they formulate their own reaction based on that perceived relationship. A particularly popular sentiment in the comments — based on the perception of that context — is that

Cooper died 'doing what he loved', i.e. 'making people laugh'. Others, though, dissent:

> To all those people saying that this was a beautiful way to go for him because he 'died doing what he loved':
> Dude...
> His heart went into cardiac arrest at a too young age. It hurts like hell and the last thing on your mind would be 'gee well at least people laugh instead of help'. He could have been saved but people weren't aware of what's happening, otherwise he could have done what he loved a whole lot longer. This death is a damn tragedy, let's not romanticise it.

Even if we don't demand that those watching should have realised what was happening and gone to help him, it's still possible, it seems, that we might be upset by the spectacle of a crowd laughing at a dying man. 'Jayden Vlogz' finds the footage 'so sad because he died and they were laughing'. In thinking about the laughter of that crowd, we are reading that crowd's reading of Cooper's body, and it seems it's eminently possible to read this reading in different ways: they should have done something to help; it is nice that they laughed; it is sad that they laughed.

We can talk about the affective value of the performer's body, then, and we can also talk about the affective value of the audience's treatment of that performer. In the particular case of Tommy Cooper's on-stage heart attack, we're also required to make an ethical judgement about our own act of bearing witness to the entire spectacle. When the footage was first uploaded to Youtube in 2009 several news outlets reported on the 'storm' that it provoked, with many of them quoting the Conservative MP Philip Davies, who was at the time a member of the House of Commons Culture, Media and Sport Select Committee. 'Most people', he said, would find the video 'tasteless':

Everybody knows he died on stage. I don't think we need to see this to be reminded of that. They ought to have some regard to his family. It does YouTube a discredit. If they have decided that this is the sort of material that people should be free to watch then I think they should reconsider.[7]

Some of those commenting on the footage when it was uploaded again later on Youtube seem to have been similarly troubled by its being so freely available: 'N Shaw' says baldly: 'This should be removed. In very poor taste.' 'This is messed up,' reads one comment; another, 'This is horrifying'; another, 'hard to watch', rounding off the comment with a crying emoji.

As the comments swirl around the footage of Cooper's falling and then prone body, it's hard to pin down the precise source of people's disquiet. Perhaps it's 'hard to watch' because it's simply very distressing for any spectator who watches another person in the middle of some kind of traumatic episode. Yet the vagueness of what 'this' is — 'This is messed up'; 'This is horrifying' — hints that our analysis of what's upsetting here needs to encompass the role of the spectators in the theatre too, and perhaps also our own role as spectators here, now, watching on Youtube and subsequently discussing what we're watching. *This* discussion right now, is — in its way — horrifying, 'messed up'. To this end, using Tommy Cooper's on-stage death as a case study serves to highlight two things. First, it reminds us that terming a spectacle 'hard to watch' may actually mean that we're talking about a subject of such extremity that 'hard to watch' is fundamentally euphemistic; indeed, throughout this book we'll encounter other phrases, 'upsetting', say, 'discomforting', or 'distressing', (or others similar) which very often bely the seriousness of the spectacle that they're applied to. Second, that formulation 'hard to watch' points up how theatrical spectacle is founded upon a basic reflexivity: it's hard to isolate the question of whether it's *proper* to show something from our discussions of how it affects spectators. When the MP Philip Davies argued that the footage of Cooper's death shouldn't be showcased online, he remarked that Youtube's decision 'that this is the sort of material that people should be free to watch' ought to have been reconsidered. Though this might just about pass as a point of propriety — an assertion that some sights are so taboo that nobody ought to be 'free to watch' them — it's made with reference to the idea that people should be reasonably permitted *not* to have to watch: 'they ought', Davies says, 'to have some regard to his family'. In other words, a) we might have to acknowledge that some spectators, like Cooper's family, might be so involved in what's seen on stage that it can be recognised as unbearably 'hard to watch', and b) the action of others watching *and watching in a particular way* might compound the pain felt by those people.

A person falls down in front of us, then, and in that moment their body is inscrutable — radically so. When scanning the comments underneath Youtube footage of Tommy Cooper dying it's remarkable how various the different possible readings are — each different comment positing its own take on the affective value of the physical event recorded on camera, and each offering a different interpretation (in more or less explicit terms) of the affective value of that event's overall context (its being watched by those in the theatre; its being watched by us). It's striking that these different interpretations do not co-exist peaceably. Take, for instance, 'Stephen Goddard', who tells us he has chosen to stop the video, affirming 'if you enjoy this you have no respect for yourself, or empathy'; evaluate that alongside the pithy rejoinder from 'rob b', who says 'whoop de doo for you mr high and mighty.. now go fuck yourself Stephen'. Such points of contention are an important reminder that we're not just considering a collection of different readings: each comment is in miniature a literary project, each constructing a representation of Cooper and of those watching him in order to assert a particular argument about how empathy functions and how it *ought* to function. The angry outbursts of ethical judgement among these comments are all bound up, then, with a process of aesthetic remaking. We've considered attempts to transform Cooper's person one way or another to suit a particular empathic model: 'his heart went into cardiac arrest... it hurts like hell' presents a very different kind of entity to a figure imagined with 'funny bones', say. But the anger stocked in many of the comments also shows us that many of those writing are picking up on attempts to transform their own person as much as Cooper's. Though 'rob b' can hardly be said to offer a constructive counter to 'Stephen Goddard' ('go fuck yourself Stephen'), his ire may have something to do with being told that he doesn't *feel* correctly (or, perhaps, doesn't feel — or is incapable of feeling — *at all*). 'If you enjoy this,' Stephen tells 'rob b' and everyone else, 'you have no respect for yourself, or empathy.' Played out in the comments below the Youtube footage, then, as much as on stage at Her Majesty's Theatre on the evening of 15 April 1984, we witness a grim kind of drama; a theatre of judgement in which onlookers compose the people they're looking at out of more or less 'funny bones', rendering them more or less thin-skinned, and more or less capable of pain.

In 2016 I started a teaching job at the University of Cambridge English Faculty, covering for a colleague who was to be engaged in a research project for the next 2 years. One of the first tasks was to write a series of lectures which might appeal to third-year students taking the Faculty's 'Tragedy' paper. As the Faculty's website tells prospective undergraduates, this paper invites students:

> to consider questions that have tested writers and artists across time: the nature of suffering; the language by which we express pain or sympathize; the ethics or cruelty of theatre.[8]

In the end I decided to put together a series concerning slapstick and tragedy. This, I thought, would require the students to think in detail about the demands made of the actor's body in various plays, as well as the audience's response to it. I would examine the physical business required of actors at key junctures in works which have been commonly accepted as tragedies, and I would ask what determined whether that physical business gave rise to tragic rather than comic effect. What, in other words, might slapstick tell us about how sympathy works?

As I began to write these lectures it began to nag at me that — when I delivered them — I'd actually be presenting, in parallel, two transactions between performer and audience. While describing, say, a blind Gloucester falling down on stage in *King Lear*, I would be occupying a stage-space of sorts myself. Indeed when I told a friend that I'd be lecturing later that term on the relationship between slapstick and tragedy she began to laugh, and said 'wouldn't it be funny if you tripped up and fell down the steps of the lecture theatre when you came in' — then, still laughing, me now laughing too — 'and *died!*' When she noticed me suddenly quiet she apologised: I wasn't, though, lost in the sad imagined spectacle of my crumpled body buried impromptu under my lecture notes (as I presume she thought I was); I was, in fact, suddenly struck by the potential of the lecture theatre as a *theatre*, a dramatic space in which I too was technically an actor and not simply an hour's worth of talk.

But for a time, I couldn't make much of the fact that I was a performer *too*, the students were an audience *too*, beyond finding it neat and quite interesting. Initially I had grand ideas of incorporating bits of physical performance into the lectures, but was, at end, too nervous to do so: having spent my own undergraduate years exploring the limits of my capacities as a diligent but ultimately rubbish actor, I thought better to accept my retirement from the profession gracefully. Insofar as I explored the lectures as performance media at all, those explorations were very limited indeed, isolated *bits* which were probably scarcely noticeable to the students. I took to wandering absent-mindedly backwards and forwards from the lectern before the lecture began, for instance, on the remote off-chance that a looker-on might find it interesting to reflect on a body shambling about a stage in front of an audience. Still more self-indulgent, in one of the lectures I talked about the slapstick tradition of throwing custard pies while holding a custard pie myself, considering the pie's facility as a slapstick weapon: far-fetched and ludicrous, perhaps, but presenting a real risk that performer and/or spectator might actually get splurged. On that occasion, I thought, there were some murmurs, some giggles, as some of the students acknowledged that I might, in theory, throw the custard pie at one of them — but for the most part, what with me lacking the confidence to invest more in such moments, these lectures didn't really offer themselves as *theatre*, and for the most part they were taken as most other lectures are, I suspect; as hour-long talks which might be more or less interesting to the hearer.

In the autumn of 2017, though, I came to think rather more carefully about the sense in which a lecturer is a performer who posits a particular kind of relationship with their audience. Midway through the term a clutch of newspapers learned that the Faculty's lecture list included, in a few cases, a small symbol next to lectures which covered potentially distressing content. But the subsequent reporting focussed on my slapstick lectures in particular, and even more particularly on one: a lecture which compared Shakespeare's treatment of sexual assault in *Titus Andronicus* with that depicted in Sarah Kane's 1996 play, *Blasted*. 'Cambridge students warned Shakespeare plays may distress them' was the *Telegraph*'s opening gambit, followed by the BBC website screenshotting the lecture's entry in the undergraduate *Notes on Courses* document and appending the headline 'Cambridge Uni students get Shakespeare trigger warnings'.[9]

The *Guardian* followed, saying 'Cambridge University issues trigger warnings for Shakespeare lecture', and the *Daily Mail's* take was forthcoming, too: '"Alas, poor snowflakes": Cambridge University issues warnings about sex and violence in Shakespeare and Greek tragedy – in case students get upset'.[10] The story travelled, and quickly: on 19 October the Fox News website said that the university had been 'slammed over Shakespeare "trigger warnings"', and Breitbart followed on 20 October, telling its visitors that 'Cambridge University issues "trigger warnings" over Shakespeare reading'.[11]

It was quickly apparent that throughout these reports, and in subsequent below-the-line comments and above-the-line opinion columns, the same few points of fascination were focussed upon and made prominent. The reports' focus on Shakespeare came to dominate over any mention of other writers, for instance: not a single reporter mentioned that other lectures concerning other writers were also marked in this way in our *Notes on Courses* document. And where early reports observed that the lecture they were talking about had examined both Shakespeare and Sarah Kane, later stories omitted Kane completely. Notable, too, was the gradual effacement of the lecture's immediate context as part of a series for that third-year tragedy paper — a paper in which students are required to study Shakespeare, and Greek tragedians like Aeschylus and Sophocles, but which also encourages them to think more broadly about tragedy as it's encountered in art and in life. So while media reports turned this single lecture into a 'Shakespeare lecture' and then by turn into Cambridge University's 'Shakespeare reading', they removed it from the company of its fellows on the tragedy paper: one lecture, for instance, considered depictions of 9/11; another considered literary representations of the Holocaust; another considered Nilüfer Demi's photograph of Alan Kurdi, the 3-year-old Syrian drowned in the Mediterranean and left on a beach in Bodrum in 2015. So some reports had begun to assert that mine was a lecture squarely and solely concerning Shakespeare — and, indeed, in some quarters, it was presented as a lecture that could stand for the university's provision of Shakespeare teaching *in toto*.

Perhaps the increasing focus on Shakespeare was to be expected. Most school curricula in the UK include some mandatory Shakespeare study; a very large proportion of the reading public will have read some Shakespeare, or will at least be familiar with something of his work. Sure enough, a significant number of online comments exhibited a prior acquaintance with his plays: 'I really never have enjoyed King Lear, I think it is really bleak'; 'Actually its The Merchant of Venice that I find difficult to watch'; 'I tremble to think what will happen if they ever have to read "Titus Andronicus"!'; 'We were reading these plays and performing these plays when I was a teenager at school. Didn't bother me and didn't upset me.'[12] Inasmuch that the story was presented in most outlets as the latest instalment in what have come to be termed 'culture wars', journalists may have found it particularly useful that Shakespeare study constituted a battleground which most readers have accessed before:

> FFS, if you've got as far as university education, don't tell me you've lived your snowflake youth completely oblivious to these Shakespeare plays and their content!! How is that possible, unless you've never been to school, never seen TV, a newspaper, a magazine, a book, or heard anyone discussing Shakespeare, duh?![13]

That Sarah Kane was increasingly omitted from reports about the lecture rather altered the substance of the story, making it sound increasingly like the warning in *Notes on Courses* applied quite generally to 'gore', rather than — more specifically — to dramatic presentations of sexual assault. But if we assume that Kane dropped out of the reports because of journalistic tidying up — as part of an overall effort designed to convey the gist of the story in a succinct, maximally accessible way — we might note how that came to consolidate Shakespeare's status as a kind of cultural obligation; studying him is required of us all. Again, online comments seemed to bear this out: 'I had Macbeth "thrust" at me at the tender age of 14 at school, and I don't think it did me any harm,' one reader noted on the *MailOnline* website; another added, 'I'm just waiting for the time when students of Shakespeare who might be easily upset are offered an option to only study the comedies instead of the likes of MacBeth or King Lear,' before arguing, 'it's time to stop accommodating the snowflakes and teach the subject as it should be taught. Anyone who doesn't want to do that is free to leave at any time.'[14] Having dropped Kane from the narrative and fogged the lecture's particular focus on sexual assault, many stories drew the grumbles of readers who sketched out rather quaint caricatures of lazy students spending all their 'university grants' on booze rather than going to lectures. The conclusions were clear: *we* sat through Shakespeare classes, and so should *they*.

While a few reports mentioned the lecture's focus on Kane's work, barely any mentioned its interest in slapstick. Again, this omission altered the story in an important way. The offending warning symbol was suggested to lecturers in cases where 'teaching contains material that could be considered upsetting (such as accounts of violence, abuse etc) *and it is not immediately obvious to the reader that this could be the case*' [my emphasis]. In a lecture series titled 'The Limits of Slapstick', it wasn't, of course, immediately obvious that theatrical enactments of rape would crop up alongside instances of clowning and excerpts from Chaplin films; alongside scenes from *Titus Andronicus*, yes, but also alongside scenes from *The Comedy of Errors*. More importantly, I had felt that the form of the works considered (and the form of the lecture itself) had the potential to be particularly challenging to sexual assault victims, more, perhaps, than the content of the plays and the content of the discussion. In examining the ways in which dramatists like Kane and Shakespeare staged sexual assault, the lecture looked in particular at cruelly slapstick dramatic techniques: it considered instances when rape was presented in a frivolous or vindictively comic way, as ridiculous; something that could or even *should* be laughed at.

Why, then, did some media outlets ignore the fact that slapstick was under discussion at the same time as sexual assault? In some stories the slapstick angle was concertedly rubbed out: the BBC website, for instance, cropped their screenshot of *Notes on Courses* so as to omit the title of the lecture series (along with its overview, which said that the series would 'examine some of the means by which dramatists have tested and exploited the actor's body for variously comic or tragic effect'). The vexed relationship between atrocity and the ridiculous was thus passed over by most reports. The lecture on *Blasted* and *Titus* did not just talk about 'gore' or 'sex', but showed how the bodies of sexual assault victims were turned into ridiculous objects and held up for mockery — as when the rapists Demetrius and Chiron goad their victim, Lavinia, whose hands they have cut off and tongue cut out:

Demetrius: So, now go tell, an if thy tongue can speak,
Who 'twas that cut thy tongue and ravished thee.
Chiron: Write down thy mind, bewray thy meaning so,
An if thy stumps will let thee, play the scribe.
Titus Andronicus (2.4.1-4)

Robbed of her voice and physical agency, Lavinia is both mocked and rendered unable to escape that mocking attention: 'an 'twere my case, I should go hang myself,' says Chiron, Demetrius joking: 'If thou had hands to help thee knit the cord.' (2.4.9-10)[15] My lecture also looked at instances in *Blasted* where another victim of sexual assault, Cate, is similarly rendered physically powerless in front of us. When pointing a gun at her rapist, for instance, she begins to stutter, and then falls abruptly to the floor:

> **Ian:** You don't want an accident. Think about your mum. And your brother. What would they think?
> **Cate:** I d- d- d- d- d- d- d- d- d- d- d- d- d-
> **Cate** *trembles and starts gasping for air.*
> *She faints.*[16]

From a position of power over her attacker, Cate is suddenly and unexpectedly dropped to the floor. Here again the victim is turned into a kind of prop, as Ian *'lies her on the bed on her back... puts the gun to her head, lies between her legs, and simulates sex.'* Then, *'as he comes,* Cate *sits bolt upright with a shout'*:

> *She laughs and laughs and laughs until she isn't laughing any more, she's crying her heart out.*
> *She collapses again and lies still.* **(p. 27)**

Sexual assault isn't permitted in these scenes to be lingered on as a serious subject or an event of dominating importance. Indeed part of what makes these plays so unsettling is that neither really affords these characters a sustained attention to how they now *feel*. Both Cate and Lavinia are put through a frenetic series of undignified actions; Cate scrabbling up and falling down, sitting bolt upright, laughing uncontrollably; Lavinia chasing after her terrified nephew, tracing words in the dust with a stick held between her wrists, and, at one point, carrying her father's lopped hand off-stage in her mouth.

Deliberately or not, other victims of sexual assault were also made to seem ridiculous in the opinion columns and online comments that came buzzing out of the reports on the lecture and its appended warning. In the *Observer* the comedian and actor David Mitchell wrote:

English literature undergraduates are being protected from the knowledge of, among other things, what one of Shakespeare's plays is about, in case it upsets them. Will budding physicists soon be allowed to shield themselves from the shocking understanding of what a black hole really is, or what will happen to the Earth when the sun explodes?[17]

After I submitted a response explaining what the lecture had been about, Mitchell apologised. But his initial sardonic tone was, by that time, part of a sardonic chorus. Comments on the *MailOnline*'s version of the story might have been cribbed from Mitchell's drafts: 'if there are warnings such as these for EngLit students, what on earth are they telling students of veterinary medicine?!'; 'What do they do to protect the medical students?' This was a popular theme: 'Well, they'd better not join any of the emergency services, the NHS, the Armed Forces or work with sharp implements'; 'Why do we have soldiers? They may get upset in battle. Why are we having doctors and nurses? Blood is scary.'[18] None of these analogies capture what might be particularly troubling to a victim of sexual assault in these cases: to consider afresh (and unexpectedly) the enactment of a rape victim's loss of personal agency. In that regard, too, the notion that I ought to subject that person to a discussion of those enactments without putting them in a position to at least imply their consent — thereby robbing them of personal agency myself — seemed to me wholly unacceptable. That I'd be discussing these enactments as potentially flippant — and even something that might be laughed at — risked further domineering over that person in the audience: do *I* get to decide how comparable a depicted trauma is with someone's real trauma?

But these online responses to the lecture alert us again to the fact that there's no easy boundary between tragedy and comedy. Throughout *Titus Andronicus* and *Blasted*, we're reminded how laughter can be cruel, or unsettling, misplaced and inappropriate; that it can be a tool of alienation rather than community. When Titus learns that his sons have been killed he begins to laugh, baffling those around him:

> **Titus:** Ha, ha, ha!
> **Marcus:** Why dost thou laugh? It fits not with this hour.
> **(3.1.263-4)**

Similarly, Cate's laughter in *Blasted* may make us laugh too, because of its sheer extremity and incongruity (*'She laughs and laughs and laughs'*); but soon she too is rendered frighteningly opaque to those watching (*'until she isn't laughing any more, she's crying her heart out. She collapses again and lies still'*). When we talk about slapstick, our alienation from such bodies as these might be construed as something reassuring: the bodies generate comic effect (rather than troubling sympathy) because they do not appear to be *real*. As Alex Clayton muses in his book *The Body in Hollywood Slapstick*:

> How do I know that the body of another is not entirely unlike my own — say, rubbery and numb rather than fleshy and sensitive? The seed of doubt raised by such questions…is a matter repeatedly circled around and played upon in physical comedy.[19]

And yet clearly Shakespeare and Kane are troubling the potential for laughter-response in these instances. Here too the bodies of the actors are presented as being unlike our own — whether laughing or falling down, they seem to be moved by inexplicable means. But if this can be thought of as physical comedy at all, it's a very unsettling kind of comedy. Insofar as these bodies behave unlike our own, that difference is not reassuring but rather estranging and isolating, even confrontational.

Blogging about the lecture for *The Oldie*, James Pembroke talked his readers through an 'excellent student production' of *The Bacchae* which he enjoyed with his son. Following the performance, he says:

> there were no gasps, no screams, and no requests for post-traumatic counselling. Uniformed sixth-formers tripped happily back on to their coach.
>
> Could it just be that school children know better than Cambridge dons that a play is all about pretending, that it might just be allegorical?[20]

A full knowledge that something isn't real doesn't preclude being profoundly affected by it, of course. And, as I'll show in the chapters that follow, slapstick particularly troubles the simplistic view that 'a play is all about pretending'. In his book *Comedy is a Man in Trouble,* Alan Dale remarks that though slapstick is 'often considered the most outrageous of comic styles':

> relying as much as it does on such ineluctable forces as gravity, momentum, and bodily functions, it's the most necessarily rooted in physical actuality.[21]

Meanwhile, in *Slapstick! The Illustrated History of Knockabout Comedy*, Tony Staveacre describes a similarly tremulous boundary between reality and pretence; in his view, slapstick is driven by:

> Violence – or the parody of violence. There's a delicate distinction. The 'injury laugh' must always be carefully calculated: if a blow seems to cause real pain, there will, usually, be no laughter.[22]

That 'delicate distinction' is delicate indeed. Even in these descriptions there's no obvious division between what's real and what's not; consider, for example, how Staveacre considers a blow that *'seems* to cause *real* pain'. Pembroke asserts that 'a play is all about pretending': why not say, rather more simply, that 'a play is pretend'? Perhaps because he knows that in *The Bacchae* Euripides shows how performance can have real and traumatic effect: Pentheus, spying on the secret ritual of the Bacchantes, ends up dressing in their clothes and being mocked by them, before being ripped apart as part of the ritual, a spectator who becomes a participant. There were 'no requests for post-traumatic counselling' following this performance of *The Bacchae*, Pembroke tells us — but in the chapters that follow I'll suggest that by thinking harder about post-traumatic states (and features of post-traumatic counselling), we can better understand how drama as an art-form is uniquely able to *involve* its viewers in the action it presents — in particularly powerful and, sometimes, particularly painful ways.

In the chapters that follow we'll see that Euripides and many other playwrights were quite aware that knowing an event is only a *performance* doesn't prevent us taking into account the ethical problems of that performance. I see an actor being forced to perform certain actions — why? How do I feel about that? How do *they* feel about that? Or: something challenging is being performed for me (or *at* me) — why? How much — and in what way — have I consented to this? Such questions might unsettle me, or anger me, and they might hurt me, revisiting upon me a traumatic experience — and none of those questions are ameliorated by my knowing that the story being acted out is only a performance. None of these questions are made easier by somebody telling me, simply, that the performance is *not real*.

I'm a student of English literature: my training, such as it is, has been devoted mostly to analysing how writers have written what they've written, and over the years I've tended to be most interested in how writers have written for performances in the theatre. Yet the reporting of my lectures on slapstick — and the responses to that reporting — reminded me that drama can't be neatly hived off from the world in which it's performed. Where I'd initially found slapstick an interesting technique for writers who used it to question the reality or contrivance of their drama, I now realised how different notions of 'reality' were being asserted and policed by a range of different commentators outside the theatre. What constitutes the 'real world' for the commenter who wrote mournfully; 'Go to university, where you are taught to be divorced from **the real world...'?** Read another comment — shared by a user called 'Mr Babbage', who lives in Switzerland — and the real world sounds like a weather front sweeping westwards across Europe: 'Oh dear little snowflakes: the real world is fast approaching. How are you going to deal with all that nastiness?'[23] David Mitchell's *Observer* column was constructed around a similar refrain, headlined 'The trouble with getting lost in your own world' and sub-headlined 'Protecting students from "distressing" plays and hi-tech targeted ads further removes us from a shared sense of what is real'; it grumbled that these warnings were obliging people who wanted 'to be able to curate their experience of the world to exclude elements they'd rather didn't exist'.

Given the material I was looking at with the students in my lectures, it seemed very clear to me that this welter of online comment was tending to think of the relationship between dramatic representation and the real the wrong way round. Put trigger warnings on lectures? Well, then, said one reader, 'they better trigger warn real life: sex, violence, taxes, bills, hard work, early mornings. It's like really hard!!'[24] But for the person who has been raped in real life, perhaps one of the challenges posed by a performance considering the subject — whether a play or a lecture — lies precisely in its constructedness; somebody who has experienced real trauma is confronted with a simulation of that trauma. 'Newsflash', remarks one below-the-line commentator: 'It's called ACTING...' Another:

> Aw. Diddums. Did the nasty fictional play upset you? *Fictional' : Not true. * 'Play' : Not real.[25]

But what exactly is going on when we simulate the traumatic experiences of others? What exactly are we doing when we insist that they sit through that simulation? What are the grounds on which I can demand that they find my deconstruction of such a simulation coldly, critically *interesting*?

Of the news that some lectures at the Cambridge English Faculty had warning symbols appended to them, one *MailOnline* reader remarked that 'it's time to stop accommodating the snowflakes and teach the subject as it should be taught', adding 'anyone who doesn't want to do that is free to leave at any time'.[26] But the *Mail*'s columnist A. N. Wilson drew a firmer line:

> At one of the most dreadful moments of King Lear, in which we have watched untold horror, a son tells his father who has had his eyes gouged out: 'Men must endure their going hence, even as their coming hither.'...If we can not 'endure' reading or studying such works, how can we be expected to endure the very real tragedies which afflict our world — and to do so with the dignity of those we most admire?[27]

Wilson's injunction that we *endure* dramatic works 'with the dignity of those we most admire' is perhaps something of a get-out clause for the *Daily Mail*: after all, it has a rich tradition of publishing theatre reviews which have marvelled that audience members didn't leave before the end of productions that they don't like. Writing about the 1995 production of *Blasted* — in a now often-referenced review titled 'This Disgusting Feast of

Filth' — Jack Tinker observed that:

Only one person left the arena during these gratuitous scenes which must say a great deal for the politeness and stoicism of British audiences.[28]

Responding to a 2010 production of the play, Quentin Letts, Tinker's successor, provided a roll call of people who he said probably liked it: the 'Loony Left', a notional 'grooved-up teacher', 'go-ahead Germans' and 'Internationalists'. The play, he notes, includes:

crazed drinking of neat alcohol, the sucking-out of human eyes, an explosion, racism, descriptions of adult violence to children, and a man being suspended by his testicles.
It could have been worse. He could have been forced to watch this baloney.[29]

In 2016, reviewing a production of *Cleansed*, Kane's third play, Letts repeated the joke:

'Death isn't the worst they can do to you,' someone says. Yes. They could make you watch a Sarah Kane play.[30]

Letts relies on hyperbole on both of the occasions when he makes his joke; nevertheless, equating the theatre-space to an inescapable place of torture acknowledges the very real way in which dramatic performance can affect and afflict a spectator.
Indeed for Letts (talking of a play that forces itself upon him), for Tinker (talking of the theatre-space as 'the arena') *and* for Wilson (talking of theatre as endurance), it seems indisputable that drama can do damage. For Letts, being 'forced to watch' *Blasted* is not a feat of worthwhile 'endurance', because Kane's plays are 'baloney'; she is not among those writers 'we most

admire', to borrow A. N. Wilson's phrase — or she *shouldn't* be. That this is 'baloney' is perhaps especially problematic, though: for all these commentators, the permissibility of the pain done to the spectator is contingent upon a qualitative judgement to do with the *form* of the drama as much as its content. All of these commentators — Wilson, Tinker, Letts — take it upon themselves to decide when it's acceptable for a spectator to get up and leave, and when it's proper that they be made to stay. Like the *MailOnline* reader outraged by the warnings on my lecture, who insisted that I should 'teach the subject as it should be taught', the commentators pronounce on the propriety of people leaving 'the arena' based on the manner in which they think the subject should be conveyed. The subject matter itself only makes up part of this judgement: for these commentators, the mode of its performance is also an important factor — perhaps, in its way, more important. Forcing unpleasant feelings upon a spectator is one matter, but these readings of performer-spectator power dynamics are also concerned that such an act of force should fit a particular stylistic template. The ramifications of these views in terms of performance and pedagogical ethics are significant, but they are views which set themselves out to begin with as literary-critical positions.

This book tries to make some sense of two, intertwined narratives. One concerns the *stuff* of my lectures on slapstick and sympathy: charting how dramatists explore and exploit the bodies of their actors in order to estrange a spectator from those bodies or to encourage that spectator's identification with them. In some respects this is a straightforwardly literary discussion. Does Shakespeare want us to sympathise entirely with the story of *King Lear*, as Samuel Johnson did in 1765, for example?

> I was many years ago so shocked by Cordelia's death, that I know not whether I ever endured to read again the last scenes of the play till I undertook to revise them as an editor.[31]

Or does he alienate us from the action in front of us, requiring us to acknowledge, as Charles Lamb did in 1811, that this is a story being staged for us?

To see Lear acted, to see an old man *tottering about the stage* with a walking stick, turned out of doors by his daughters in a rainy night, has nothing in it but what is painful and disgusting [my emphasis].[32]

But this sort of literary discussion gives rise to wider, sociological questions when we consider the second narrative: that of the ways in which these lectures themselves were presented, received, reported and discussed. Here, as in dramatic scripts and performances, people came to be presented (and understood) as more or less slapstick and more or less sympathetic figures, their situations more or less to be laughed at, and more or less to be endured. Alongside performances staged at the Globe or the Gate, then, I'll also be analysing the dramatic situations acted out in other arenas which are, I suppose, only theatres in a more figurative sense: the comment threads which trail below Youtube videos and online opinion columns.

The next three chapters each begin by considering a particular trope associated with slapstick modes of performance. The next chapter ('Falling Down'), for instance, considers one of the most basic demonstrations of comic physical drama: the moment of falling, when the performer's body is abruptly removed from their control. Chapter 3, 'Slosh', begins with a consideration of the clown's arsenal of weapons: custard pies, buckets of water and of flour, and indeed the 'slap stick' itself — some of the means by which a slapstick performer might simulate violence against another. Chapter 4, 'No Two Alike', opens with a consideration of 'the mirror scene' and situations of confusing, interchangeable likeness more generally. By examining these tropes I analyse the literary and dramatic strategies by which writers and performers style human bodies as *slapstick* bodies; variously unfeeling, unthinking, puppeted or automatic entities. The final chapter, 'Thaw', would seem at first glance to take leave of literary study entirely: it engages instead with the discussions of perceived 'snowflakery' which take place online on platforms like Breitbart or *MailOnline*, and in pieces of writing which are styled as more or less academic works of social commentary. Breitbart users called 'Freethinker' or 'Red Pilled Thoughtcrimes' might not consider themselves dramatists, of course, and nor necessarily would the Breitbart and *Spectator* columnist James Delingpole (a self-described 'writer, blogger, podcaster, entertainer and troublemaker'), or Milo Yiannopoulos (a self-styled 'journalist, author, pundit…a provocateur, a crusader, and an entertainer'), or Greg Lukianoff ('the head of the Foundation for Individual Rights in Education') or Jonathan Haidt (a 'social psychologist' and 'a professor at New York University's Stern School of Business').[33] All of them, though, deploy similar techniques in their writing in order to control the bodies of the people they write about, managing their readers' empathetic posture in relation to those people.

At heart, then, this is a study which is interested, primarily, in techniques of dramatic performance and dramatic framing. Speaking not long after *Blasted* had premiered, Kane pointed out that the play received more media coverage than the actual rape and murder of a teenage girl, and said: 'The thing that shocks me most is that the media seem to have been more upset by the representation of violence than by violence itself.'[34] And yet this seems a touch disingenuous: presumably she sought some particular effect when she situated the actions represented in *Blasted* within an inescapable theatrical space, *representing* violence rather than simply directing us with description towards the 'real' thing. However it works, this is the unique power of drama; realised in the moment the body of an actor stands before us; the revolutionary moment which we were told first happened in ancient Athens. Formerly, Diogenes Laertius tells us, 'in tragedy the chorus was the only actor' (they came forth 'and sang to the gods', according to another commentator) — but then, 'in order to give the chorus breathing space', 'Thespis devised a single actor'.[35] Our talk nowadays of 'snowflakes' might seem something new; indeed as of January 2018 the Oxford English Dictionary only had a draft addition to their definition of the term:

> (usually derogatory and potentially offensive). Originally: a person, esp. a child, regarded as having a unique personality and potential. Later: a person mockingly characterized as overly sensitive or easily offended, esp. one said to consider himself or herself entitled to special treatment or consideration.[36]

According to the OED, the term 'alludes in earliest use' — reckoned to be 1983 — 'to the notion that no two snowflakes are identical, later to their pristine or fragile condition'. And yet, as this book will make clear, we have used the theatre for centuries to challenge ourselves to think through these judgements: to look at a figure in front of us and to wonder how much they are like us, and how much we stand apart from them.

> Pathetic wasters, melt away you oxygen thieves...
> '**Sir Pat**', Pontefract, United Kingdom, comment on 'Alas, poor snowflakes: Cambridge University issues warning about sex and violence in Shakespeare and Greek tragedy – in case students get upset', *MailOnline*, 18 October 2017

> Oh that this too, too sallied flesh would melt,
> Thaw, and resolve itself into a dew...
> **William Shakespeare**, *Hamlet* (1.2.129-30)

Cate *begins to tremble.* **Ian** *is laughing.*

Cate *faints.*

Ian *stops laughing and stares at her motionless body.*

Sarah Kane, *Blasted* (p. 9)

Chapter 2

Falling Down

Tragedy is often described as a kind of falling. Dr Faustus contracts his soul to Satan in exchange for four-and-twenty years of power, and — time up — he is ripped apart by devils: the chorus instructs us to 'Regard his hellish fall,/Whose fiendful fortune may exhort the wise/Only to wonder at unlawful things'.[1] Satan himself is understood to have fallen from heaven with his devils ('the companions of his fall', as John Milton puts it in *Paradise Lost*).[2] When we chart an individual's trajectory from a figuratively high state to a low one, it seems it's particularly helpful to conceive of it as a literal kind of falling. Consider this translation of Aristotle's *Poetics*, a treatise on tragic theatre originally written 3 centuries BC:

it should be an imitation of events that evoke fear and pity, since that is the distinctive feature of this kind of imitation. So it is clear first of all that decent men should not be seen **undergoing a change from good fortune to bad fortune** — this does not evoke fear or pity, but disgust. Nor should depraved people be seen **undergoing a change from bad fortune to good fortune** — this is the least tragic of all: it has none of the right effects, since it is neither agreeable, nor does it evoke pity or fear. **Nor again should a very wicked person fall from good fortune to bad fortune**...[3]

In the original Greek, these three examples of transition are described using the same word, μεταβάλλω — 'metaballo'. This is variously defined as a kind of change or transformation; in some definitions, it involves a particular quality of abruptness. In that regard, the English word 'fall' is very appealing to a translator; if you were finding that formulation 'undergoing a change' a little repetitious, 'fall' seems a very reasonable, even preferable alternative.

Falling is an abrupt movement from high to low: literally and (often) metaphorically too. But the idea of falling comes with connotations which aren't so pronounced in notions of 'transforming', or 'changing' (or however else we might want to translate μεταβάλλω). When we fall our condition changes abruptly, and it also changes in a way that's outside of our control. Succumbing to gravity we do not just fall, we become endowed with a quality of *having fallen*. In *Paradise Lost*, Beelzebub can barely recognise Satan now he's been cast out of heaven:

O how fallen! how changed
From him, who in the happy realms of light
Clothed with transcendent brightness didst outshine
Myriads though bright
Paradise Lost (1.84-7)

In musing about the most effective forms of tragedy, Aristotle considers conceptual ups and downs when he thinks of the routes which are most likely to 'evoke fear and pity' rather than 'disgust'. The reactions of the onlooker, he says, will depend on the ethical or social starting position of the individual: are we watching people who start high, as 'decent men', or low, as 'depraved people'? But when we think about falling in more literal, more physical terms, we might find that our practices of fear, pity or disgust can sometimes be conducted separately from our judging the victim to be more or less ethically deserving of it. The spectacle of Satan prostrate in the early books of *Paradise Lost* may elicit understanding from us (if not outright sympathy) partly because he is fallible in a very physical sense: he occupies a body as we do, and something about his bodily condition can be found fearful, pitiable or disgusting irrespective of his ethical position.

But for all that we might talk of tragic falls, there is of course a very rich tradition of falling over for comic effect. In *The Body in Hollywood Slapstick*, Alex Clayton analyses a sequence from the 1938 film *Bringing Up Baby*, in which Cary Grant walks into shot only to slip up on an olive which has just been thrown away by Katharine Hepburn. It's funny, Clayton argues, because:

> The ever-present possibility of slipping on an olive is a condition of being embodied, something we all have to learn to live with. Embodiment, in this sense, suggests nothing more, or less, than the fact of having, or being, a body.[4]

Clayton argues that being suddenly and emphatically reminded of bodiliness leads to comic effect. Indeed it's possible to trace out over many centuries of art a dichotomy drawn between the comic body and a more noble, less comic *spirit*. In this way we might reflect that Milton's Satan is brought low in two respects: thrown downwards from heaven, but also contained in a trivial, base and limited body. It's notable that in his 1901 essay, 'On Laughter', the philosopher Henri Bergson described this 'condition of being embodied' in terms that are redolent of such a fall from heaven:

> The soul imparts a portion of its winged lightness to the body it animates...the immateriality which thus passes into matter is what is called gracefulness. Matter, however, is obstinate and resists. It draws to itself the ever-alert activity of this higher principle, would fain convert it to its own inertia and cause it to revert to mere automatism.[5]

While a fall from a high condition to a low one might be lamented, the physical spectacle of someone low and body-bound is more often taken to be comic, in Bergson's judgement. By using the term 'gracefulness' here, he combines an observation about our bodies with something of a spiritual appraisal, associating our human susceptibility to falling over in everyday life (slipping on olives and banana skins, tripping on paving stones, blundering backwards over the dog) with the condition of having fallen spiritually — from God and from *his* grace. We were once angelic (cavorting about in 'winged lightness'), but we fall — over and over again — because we have fallen from Paradise already.

A great many conventions of artistic and dramatic expression are described — more or less consciously — in a way that has them falling into line with Bergson's view of the body. Simon Shepherd observes how the body of the clown in performance is traditionally:

> angled at the hips, bent forward or back, arse or genitals out, knees bent, twists to the shoulders. The angles tend to be off the vertical, spines curved, shoulders rarely horizontal; the centre of gravity has to be low enough to allow bent knee postures.[6]

He contrasts this with illustrations of courtly dancers, whose bodies 'are vertical. The limbs of the masque dancers conform to geometric patterns, imaging cosmic order; what they do is not a picture of geometry but geometry itself, abstract.' Clowns, by resisting geometric patterns, stick in the craw of this perceived cosmic order. When Barbara Ravelhofer quotes the choreographer Fabritio Caroso's 'deep suspicions of knees spread too far apart as if "to urinate"', we can see how different forms of lowness are neatly aligned: figures which are 'off the vertical' resist geometry, order, balance and gracefulness; they are impelled towards the scatalogical; they are to be understood as comic; in sum, as Shepherd puts it, they 'might be said to be not only low in physical terms, but morally "low"'.[7] When watching a performance these associations may be made almost without thinking, or they may relate in a way that we read as an intelligible story: a noble figure is brought low for instance, or a base character is locked in his or her bodily urges, or a figure disrupts social or natural orders with their actions.

When watching a human body collapsing to the floor — whether inside a theatre or outside it — an onlooker is regarding a site which is capable of many different possible readings. Perhaps it can be used to chart in crude, literal terms a metaphorical loss of social standing: a fall might be read as a straightforward and localised loss of dignity, or perhaps it also indicates a more general loss of social standing, an invitation to note that this person's life now accommodates the possibility of sprawling on the floor where it did not before. Perhaps, by seeing it fall, the spectator recognises with a jolt that this is a body subject to physical law: not just an avatar, a hypothetical figure in a hypothetical situation, but a body subject to gravity, to bruising, to bleeding, to breaking. Or perhaps it's better to say that the falling body demands the spectator's scrutiny, asking: *is* that body subject to all the same laws which govern the spectator's own? Because as we'll see, in that moment of another person's body seeming to lose control of itself, it's not a given that the spectator finds that body consonant with their own: sympathy for someone falling over is sometimes superseded by a response founded on the belief that the fallen person is in some way alien. The falling body can be reframed so that we read it as qualitatively *unlike* our own body.

In 2010 the UK's then Minister for Education, Michael Gove, was walking to a Cabinet meeting. Carrying an umbrella in his right hand and holding a folder of papers in his left, TV cameras caught the moment when his feet suddenly slid from under him, his legs crumpled and he landed on his arse on the pavement. He gets up, turns to look accusingly at the pavement, and carries on his way. The reporters call to him, and he smiles, laughs a little and begins to walk a little stiffly. Watching the footage back, you'll hear the following from the onlookers:

'Wheeeey!'

and

'Are you okay, sir?'

Those two responses hold Gove's body in tension between two states.[8] It is addressed first as a cipher in a comic formula. 'Wheeeey!' shout the reporters, as they would if someone dropped a glass in a pub. The call is taken up in the comments underneath the video:

The most elegant treatment of Gove's body as a prop in a comic 'bit' is perhaps to be found in an earlier comment, where one user, calling themselves 'Nelson Muntz' after the schoolboy bully in *The Simpsons*, quoted Muntz's catchphrase:

Rather brilliantly, 'Nelson Muntz' appears to have no other registered activity on Youtube (in other words, somebody seems to have registered the account on Youtube solely for this purpose). But the performance of this comment doesn't just register the user's amusement at Gove's misfortune; it asserts that the situation (Gove's misfortune *and* the spectator's gloating amusement) is a replicable trope. Furthermore, 'Nelson Muntz' delivers that assertion with a touch of intertextual panache:

Gove's fall is rendered equivalent to, say, Grandpa Simpson's trousers falling down (in season 2 episode 20, 'The War of the Simpsons'), or the geek Martin Prince having his swimming trunks ripped off in season 6 episode 1, 'Bart of Darkness'. (There are many other similar examples to be found across the 29 current seasons of *The Simpsons*.)

A significant number of viewers treat Gove's body as a simple point in an endlessly repeatable comic sequence, and many of them find pleasure in this. 'Whenever I'm sad I just come back to this video and suddenly everything feels better,' says one user, for instance; another says, 'Always cheers me up this video does!'; 'I must go to bed,' another ruminates, 'I've been watching this for 3 hours.' Versions of the same video have been created which show the fall on a loop: searching for 'Michael Gove falls over' will also yield 'Ten minutes of Gove falling over (Eminem remix)' and 'Michael Gove falls over-and-over-and-over (and over).' But something is ignored if we treat the fall as endlessly repeatable. Consider again this question, from Alex Clayton:

> How do I know that the body of another is not entirely unlike my own — say, rubbery and numb rather than fleshy and sensitive? The seed of doubt raised by such questions ...is a matter repeatedly circled around and played upon in physical comedy.[9]

'Are you okay, sir?' This question, in counterpoint to the 'wheeeey!' of the other reporters, acknowledges that Gove's body might not be rubbery and numb. The slight stiffening of his gait as he continues on his way suggests some physical hurt, or — possibly — embarrassment. Either way, and no matter how mild, the fall has evidently done this figure some harm.

When I first saw the video of Michael Gove falling over, I laughed. I may, I suppose, have said 'wheeeey!' — I don't recall. Like a great many people who work in education, I found that I had disagreed with most of what Michael Gove did as Education Secretary, and so I was delighted to see him looking silly and rather powerless. Sharing this video on Facebook would go down well with my friends, I thought, many of whom also worked in education and many of whom also considered him bad at his job. I only got as far as copying and pasting the link into a Facebook status, though. After watching the video through a couple more times, I deleted the status, finding that, on balance, the figure in the video was eliciting my sympathy more than my amusement. This wouldn't do at all, I concluded: it would complicate my objections to Gove's policies too much if I posted manifest evidence that he was a person capable of falling over like any other idiot — like me or you.

Thinking through Gove's pratfall is instructive on a few different counts, then. First, it's clear that there is not always a fixed distinction between sympathy and amusement. In the same way, there's no easy way of deciding if the body that we're looking at is 'rubbery and numb' *or* 'fleshy and sensitive'. Gove slipping over is an acute example of how we might understand that 'or' to be 'repeatedly circled around and played upon' (as Clayton puts it) in a mode that we tend to interpret as 'physical comedy'. And even though Gove's fall wasn't undertaken with an audience in mind, the footage of it has come to be curated, framed and serially reframed. I, no less than the Youtuber who dubbed a 10-minute Eminem track over the footage, was curating the spectacle of Gove's tumble, choosing to present it (or not to present it) according to a particular, hoped-for effect.

Many, many people have watched the footage of Gove falling over (taking into account the various edits and remixes of it on Youtube, it's been viewed more than 750,000 times at time of writing). Every person who has watched Michael Gove fall over will have made a decision about how to read that fall, to see him as more or less rubbery and numb, more or less fleshy and sensitive. The medium has turned his fall into a performance. By treating it as a performance, we have become aware of ourselves as the viewers, and have turned him into a performer: *our* performer; a performer who occupies a particular relationship with our gaze.

The best part is when he glances towards the cameras with a look of absolute fury, like the veil of his public image was snatched away for a brief unexpected moment, revealing the true malice underneath, before he catches himself and puts the facade back on, all smiles.[10]

'A glorious moment,' says 'Nicholas Collins'. 'I'm not sure what was better – the slip or his subsequent determination to act as though he wasn't embarrassed and everything was fine.' These, in essence, are sophisticated glosses on Nelson Muntz's 'ha ha': the magic of slapstick, of Gove demonstrably occupying a body, is that we can imagine ourselves into how he must have felt; at the same time, the feeling that this is a performance means we assert a form of control over him, Gove somehow knowing we are watching ('this clown performs for *me!*'). Those who puppet this poor hapless man to an Eminem track might not be said to undertake a concerted artistic project, but they are in their way responding to and enacting a recognisable set of dramatic techniques.

The Roman general Marc Antony was an impressive physical specimen. According to Plutarch, his was 'a noble presence': his 'goodly thick beard', 'broad forehead' and 'manly look' were apparently 'commonly seen in Hercules' pictures, stamped or graven in metal'. Thought by many to be descended from Hercules himself, Antony confirmed this opinion, Plutarch said, 'in all his doings' and by 'resembling him in the likeness of his body'.[11] Leafing through Shakespeare's *Antony and Cleopatra* you'll find a number of characters reaffirming the theory that

Marc Antony has inherited something of a superhuman form: he is part of the 'triple pillar of the world', described as 'the demi-Atlas of this Earth' (1.1.12; 1.5.23). When Cleopatra dreams of him she observes how 'His legs bestrid the Ocean' and 'his rear'd arm/Crested the world', noting how his voice, when raised in anger, 'was as rattling thunder' (5.2.81-2; 85).

Antony may be described in terms that liken him to a divine being, but the behaviour Shakespeare requires of his body on stage tends more towards that of Gove than Jove. See, for instance, how Antony's physical mightiness is deftly turned into a ludicrous inconvenience as Cleopatra requires that he is lifted, dying, to her embrace:

> **Antony:** I am dying, Egypt, dying. Only
> I here importune death awhile until
> Of many thousand kisses, the poor last
> I lay upon thy lips.
> **Cleopatra:** I dare not, dear.
> Dear my lord, pardon. I dare not
> Lest I be taken.
> [...]
> But come, come Antony —
> — Help me, my women! — We must draw thee up.
> Assist, good friends! [*They begin lifting* **Antony**.]
> **Antony:** Oh, quick, or I am gone.
> **Cleopatra:** Here's sport indeed. How heavy weighs my lord!
> Our strength is all gone into heaviness —
> That makes the weight. (4.15.19-24; 30-5)

Shakespeare insists that this scene should play out clumsily. Over ten lines are spoken between 'we must draw thee up' and Antony finally being permitted to rest. With remarkable clunkiness the figurative heaviness of the spectacle before us — the sadness of it — is associated, recurrently, with Antony's literal heaviness. In case we don't pick up on that association when Cleopatra notes it ('How heavy weighs my lord!/Our strength is all gone into heaviness'), other onlookers lament the 'heavy sight' (4.15.42) of Antony's death and the 'Most heavy day' of its occurrence (4.14.136). Most productions eventually reach a glorious tableau, 'a Roman by a Roman/Valiantly vanquished', recumbent and resplendent in the arms of his lover, but Shakespeare insists that his audience pay attention to the effort that goes into arranging and achieving that tableau (4.15.59-60) This means that for all of Antony's grand talk of self-will we see quite clearly that he is entirely subject to Cleopatra's stage management. This comes across in her talking over him ('Give me some wine, and let me speak a little —' 'No, let me speak, and let me rail'), but it is emphasised too by the logistical struggle involved in hefting his body to where Cleopatra wants it: she hesitates and refuses, in fact, to descend to where Antony is — 'I dare not, dear./Dear my Lord, pardon. I dare not/Lest I be taken' (4.15.22-4).

The glory of Antony's demise is significantly undercut by the treatment of his body, but it's also important to note that the simple fact of *having* a body is shown to oppose the power he claims for himself. This is recurrently emphasised by Shakespeare. Antony's last words, 'Now my spirit is going./I can no more' (4.15.60-1), seek to completely ignore the cumbersome body left behind, but Shakespeare ensures that we can't so easily ignore it: even before Cleopatra started heaving him bodily about the place, Antony had been trying (and conspicuously failing) to wish that body away. 'Thou yet behold'st me?' he asks his servant, Eros: 'Ay, noble lord,' Eros replies.

Antony: Sometime we see a cloud that's dragonish,
A vapor sometime like a bear or lion,
A towered citadel, a pendent rock,
A forkèd mountain or blue promontory
With trees upon't that nod unto the world

And mock our eyes with air. Thou hast seen these signs.
They are black vesper's pageants.
Eros: Ay, my lord.
Antony: That which is now a horse, even with a thought
The rack dislimns and makes it indistinct
As water is in water.
Eros: It does, my lord.
Antony: My good knave Eros, now thy captain is
Even such a body. Here I am Antony,
Yet cannot hold this visible shape, my knave. **(4.14.1-14)**

It's a beautiful way of saying that he's in a funk: this hard-to-pin-down image (or, rather, this hard-to-pin-down succession of images) conveying his sense of turmoil and uncertainty. But even as he *says* that he cannot hold 'this visible shape' he manifestly *is* holding it. Even while announcing its insubstantiality, these lines actually draw attention to and emphasise the presence of the actor's body on stage before us.

Shakespeare continues to demonstrate that Antony cannot escape this body, and he shows too that it's a body not under Antony's control. Asking Eros to kill him doesn't work — Eros kills himself instead — and so Antony attempts suicide:

Antony: I will be
A bridegroom in my death and run into't
As to a lover's bed. Come, then, and Eros,
Thy master dies thy scholar; to do thus
I learned of thee. [*He falls on his sword.*] How, not dead? Not dead?
The guard, ho! Oh, dispatch me! **(4.14.99-104)**

Antony is unable to die: 'let him that loves me, strike me dead,' he instructs the guards who enter, but each answers him in turn 'Not I', 'Nor I', 'Nor anyone' (108-10). But it's through the particular clumsiness of the bungled suicide that Shakespeare stresses that Antony is imprisoned not just in his situation but on stage. Other characters get to stage manage their own deaths: Cleopatra's, later, is a masterpiece of order. Or consider Othelloh, who, as T. S. Eliot believed, is *'cheering himself up'*, 'turning himself into a pathetic figure, by adopting an aesthetic rather than a moral attitude, dramatizing himself against his environment'.[12]

> **Othello:** And say, besides, that in Aleppo once,
> Where a malignant and a turbaned Turk
> Beat a Venetian and traduced the state,
> I took by th'throat the circumcisèd dog
> And smote him thus. [*He stabs himself.*] **(5.2.345-9)**

Compare where Antony's own 'thus' falls: mid-sentence, meaning he either talks, ludicrously, for another four words after stabbing himself, or that he misses out on the dramatic convergence of enactment and self-narration so grandly exhibited by Othello's 'thus'. The wrinkle between the 'thus' and the action it refers to serves as a signal that Antony's ability to write his own end is undermined by his inability to command his overall aesthetic fate.

Antony's loss of self-control is highly expressive: it encapsulates a fall from good fortune to bad fortune, and it illustrates that this so-called 'demi-Atlas' has been reduced to occupying a clumsy human form very like mine, or yours or Michael Gove's. What's more, his loss of self-control serves to illustrate who controls him when he manifestly doesn't control himself. In the world of the play he's shown to be at the mercy of the guards, say, or Cleopatra; importantly, the futile, clumsy attempt to manage the aesthetics of his body's behaviour underscores how much he's at the mercy of the author, too. Not long before he wrote *Antony and Cleopatra*, Shakespeare was arranging another character's failed suicide: in *King Lear*, the blinded Duke of Gloucester believes he is being led to the cliffs at Dover, set, he is told, 'within a foot of th'extreme verge' (4.6.27). He has been led there by his estranged son, Edgar, pretending here to be a 'bedlam beggar' named Poor Tom. Tom tells Gloucester

> The murmuring surge
> That on th'unnumbered idle pebble chafes,
> Cannot be heard so high. I'll look no more,
> Lest my brain turn and the deficient sight
> Topple down headlong. **(4.6.21-5)**

Gloucester bids 'Tom' farewell and falls forward.

> **Edgar:** Gone, sir; farewell.
> And yet I know not how conceit may rob
> The treasury of life when life itself
> Yields to the theft. Had he been where he thought,
> By this had thought been past. Alive or dead?
> Ho, you, sir! Friend, hear you, sir? Speak! –
> Thus might he pass indeed. Yet he revives.
> What are you, sir?
> **Gloucester:** Away and let me die.
> **Edgar:** Hadst thou been aught but gossamer, feathers, air,
> So many fathom down precipitating,
> Thou'dst shivered like an egg; but thou dost breathe,
> Hast heavy substance, bleed'st not, speak'st, art sound.
> Ten masts at each make not the altitude
> Which thou hast perpendicularly fell.
> Thy life's a miracle. Speak yet again.
> **Gloucester:** But have I fallen, or no? **(4.6.41-56)**

'But have I fallen, or no?' The audience are only a little less confused than Gloucester: when Edgar confides in them, 'Had he been where he *thought*,/By this had thought been passed', it's the first acknowledgement that Gloucester hasn't actually been led to the edge of a cliff. It's an extraordinary deception practised upon the onlooking audience, and in this respect would seem to align their confusion with that of Gloucester: watching this scene play out in *Lear*, we are as disorientated as the blind man prostrate on the floor. By having them attempt suicide, Shakespeare shows us the characters trying to escape the circumstances of the story. But by staging the attempts in this particularly clumsy way, he's also making the spectators note that the figures before us are being kept awkwardly on stage and under scrutiny.

The awkwardness of our scrutiny is heightened because the actor's fall is obviously bogus. Leading up to it Shakespeare has presented a pattern of equally weighted claims and counter-claims about what it is that we're supposed to be looking at: 'methinks the ground is even', Gloucester muses, for example, with Edgar countering that it's 'horrible steep'. This is only confusing because theatregoers are conditioned to prioritise the question 'what am I supposed to be looking at?' over other sensory interpretations; why shouldn't Gloucester correctly apprehend that the ground is even simply because he has lost his sight? Shakespeare's audience may swallow Edgar's explanation for this ('why, then, your other senses grow imperfect by your eyes' anguish'), but the moment of the actor's fall strains their credulity to breaking point. The mechanics of a fall onto a floor and from a great height are very different, and however the actor begins this fall — productions have had Gloucester standing, kneeling, sometimes on a low platform — it's highly challenging to fake the surprise of impact. If this is simply bad drama it's concertedly so: Shakespeare demands that the whole scene is necessarily ungraceful. Rhythmically the mutual farewell is neat and satisfactory:

Gloucester: Now, fellow, fare thee well.
Edgar: Gone, sir; farewell. **(4.6.43)**

That neatness, though, requires an awkward end-stop where we and Edgar simply have to look at Gloucester heaped on the boards.

The clumsiness of these scenes stretches the spectator's credulity, drawing attention to the overall artistic contrivance of what's presented on stage, and drawing the spectator's attention to their own ongoing act of scrutiny. In *Lear* in particular, that act of scrutiny is shown to be an oppressive, cruel force in itself. Near the play's conclusion the actor playing Cordelia is carried out into the stage-space, and the audience is told that Cordelia is dead. Within the story of the play this is an abrupt development, ruled by chance: Cordelia is dead simply because a messenger arrived too late to revoke a 'writ' on her life, failing to bring a 'token of reprieve' to her jailer in time. On stage, too — having seen just how easily Shakespeare made the actor-as-Gloucester play 'dead' and then get back up in Act 4 Scene 6 — Cordelia's death appears especially arbitrary. This is underscored as Lear addresses the body several times: 'Ha?/What is't thou sayest?', 'Why should a dog, a horse, a rat have life,/And thou no breath at all?' (5.3.45-6; 82-3) The scene flirts with the liveness of the performer by other means, too. 'Lend me a looking-glass,' Lear says to those around him;

If that her breath will mist or stain the stone,
Why then she lives. **(5.3.235-7)**

A little later Lear insists 'This feather stirs. She lives!' (239). If a mirror was held to the actor's lips, of course, it would indeed be misted; a feather would indeed stir. In the folio version of this scene the play teases the onlookers still further with Lear's last words: 'Look on her! Look, her lips,/Look there. Look there!'

(286-7) Where Shakespeare compelled the actors playing Antony and Gloucester to carry on some scenes more, here we are made aware that the actor Cordelia is not being permitted to continue.

Here Shakespeare draws our attention to what the body is doing — the actor playing Cordelia must be breathing, we know that. But he also goes to great lengths in these scenes to interrogate the very substance of these bodies. Carrying another actor onto the stage, whoever plays Lear demands that we take in the spectacle before us. The line 'howl, howl, howl, howl!' takes up time — requiring onlookers to reflect on the sadness of what they see, but also requiring that they appraise several other physical and logistical details: the actor's body has weight, it requires effort to carry it, it is flopping this way or that as it's hefted across the stage. 'Oh, you are men of stones!' Lear scolds those who are looking on, but of course this is only a figure of speech. This is yet another instance where Shakespeare juxtaposes the spectacle of bodies being conspicuously body-like (being fleshy, having mass) with someone wondering aloud what such bodies are made of: had Gloucester's falling body 'been aught but gossamer, feathers, air', it would have 'shivered like an egg' upon impact, Edgar muses earlier in *Lear*; Antony, as we have seen, compares his own body to a shape-shifting cloud moments before trying to run himself through with a sword. So while Shakespeare may use his actors' bodies to emphasise that the situation presented is *not real* — it's a story played out in a theatre — he seems at the same time to linger on the real presence and substance of those bodies.

As the actor playing Lear carries in the actor who played his daughter, the so-called 'men of stones' speak. 'Is this the promised end?' one asks; the other, the actor playing Edgar, adds the curious line 'Or image of that horror?' (237-8). That this is an *image* places the spectacle squarely in the realm of art, true: indeed, showing Cordelia cradled by her father, Lear, Shakespeare is riffing off artistic traditions of the *pietà* (many artists — Michelangelo and El Greco prominent among them — have depicted the body of Christ in the arms of his grieving mother).[13] At the same time, it's the clumsiness of the bodies within that frame which makes manifest the author's *exertion* of power over them. This is why Charles Lamb complained in 1811 that 'to see Lear acted, to see an old man tottering about the stage with a walking stick, turned out of doors by his daughters in a rainy night, has nothing in it but what is painful and disgusting'.[14] For Shakespeare, the physical facts that govern the actor's body on the stage are a crucial part of what makes the play so viscerally 'painful and disgusting': gravity, weight, gangliness, the limits of the actor's reach, strength or breath, are all — in their way — statements of that body's independence from the author's control. By showing this to be such a body, Shakespeare signals that it isn't wholly his to command while in any case presuming to command it. Forcing *this* body into the aesthetic framework he has assigned to it, Shakespeare shows us how his artistic efforts are an act of oppression.

Go back to that Youtube video, 'Michael Gove falls over', and scroll through the comments. Many wish harm upon the body which is shown falling over. Some — a few — take care to transform that figure descriptively into something that isn't made of the same stuff as we are. 'He looked like a ventriloquist dummy being dropped,' says one; another, 'Gove resembles a sperm in a suit'; 'That's what happens,' concludes another, 'when you're made of slime.' But a very sizeable number of the comments insist that Gove's body is a body which can sustain specific forms of harm, described in the meticulous detail of the physically possible; forms of harm to which we too might fall victim. Eight of the 332 comments which can be found posted underneath this video at time of writing express the wish that Gove should have broken his neck. Many others profess to wish he had died, and many of them outline specific circumstances in which he might have done so:

Why didn't he hit his head and die? Disappointed...

Olly Willers

Should have hit his head and died

Jordan

I wish there had been a rope around his neck as he went down.

salvadormarley

These comments are radical expressions of ill will. They do not seek to provide any explanation for their animus, and stand as straightforward expressions of hate. Other comments made in this vein try to incorporate and justify their ill-wishes within a notionally political thesis, as here:

I would really like them all to suffer a tragic accident that leaves them either dead or disabled. Be funnier if they were disabled and had to spend all their money on legal fees, then they'd need to claim benefits lols.

sod-off tax-dodging gits

The point here, presumably, is that the suffering visited upon Gove imaginatively is intended as redress for the suffering experienced by others because of his actions as a politician. 'Sod-off tax-dodging gits' seeks to justify wishing harm upon Gove and his colleagues by arguing that they were part of a government that inflicted great pain on disabled people, people in need of legal aid, people in need of state benefits. The argumentative strategy here is not just to draw an equivalence of harm, but to try and lift those suffering people out of the abstract and into the particular, by homing in on one particular figure: this is a way of saying 'imagine if *he* suffered as any one of them did'.

So many of the comments, though, lack even this level of sophistication. Some of the most malevolent could be seen to caper more or less unwittingly into the far-fetched and ludicrous:

I wish he'd fallen on an HIV ridden needle and dies a slow and painful AIDS death. That would have made my day.

Tasbo1982

But others insist that Gove's body should exist in a state governed by plausible physical rules, and that it should be harmed within that state. 'Pity he didn't break his neck' says one; another, 'Why didnt he die just there'. What are such writers doing when they seek to challenge the normal conventions of acceptability, energetically assaulting — in particular — the orthodox binary between the slapstick, cartoonish realm where no real harm is done, and the world in which we live? Some of the comments below the video try to describe Gove's body as unreal; others seek instead to emphasise its reality and its participation in the same physical world in which we live. Some comments wish harm upon the person they see falling before them but absolve themselves of feeling guilty about that by reformulating him as a slapstick (rubbery, numb) kind of body. Others, notably, make a point of recognising Gove's as a body which could ordinarily attract sympathetic understanding — a body like ours, in other words — *so* that they can then make a show of depriving it of sympathy.

Unlike *King Lear* or *Antony and Cleopatra*, the footage of Michael Gove's fall was not designed as an artistic product. When watching Michael Gove fall on his arse, we are not, to begin with, considering a character in a story but rather a person on a street. But, examining the ways in which Shakespeare treats the bodies of his actors in plays like *King Lear* and *Antony and Cleopatra*, it's necessary to frown a little at our distinctions between 'real' action and that which we consider *not* real. When watching the body of a performer crumple to the floor — no matter their situation in the story they participate in — we are bearing witness to an authentic physical action taking place in front of us. While we may assume qualities commonly associated with the slapstick body to be *a priori* qualities, inherently present in the mode of their performance or even in the body of the performer, the examples that we've considered in this chapter have highlighted how bodies *come to be formulated* as a slapstick body. In subjecting the bodies of the actors playing Antony, Gloucester and Cordelia to extended scrutiny, Shakespeare shows us that real physical action can be framed in such a way that the onlooker notices (perhaps even participates in) the lines of control governing the clumsy body's behaviour on stage. Reading through the many ugly comments upon footage of Michael Gove falling over, it's striking that the very substance of Gove's body is tussled over, and not just his actions. Those commenting bicker indirectly with one another about what this figure is made of: endowing the body with qualities which ratchet up or diminish its capacity for our sympathetic understanding.

As we've seen, the conventions that we associate with slapstick performance make the onlooker more aware that the author is exerting their power over the performer, because the performer's body always has encoded within it a self-evident resistance to that attempted authorial control. Even if not under the full control of its owner, the body still possesses a kind of independence from the author — obeying physics as its chief ruler over and above the desires and designs of the writer. Read Milton, or Marlowe, or Shakespeare, and we can readily enough treat the spectacle of someone falling as something literally or metaphorically intelligible within the world of the falling person's story. And, performed on stage before us, someone literally falling over alerts us to the complex interplay between what is 'real' and what might be designated fictional: it makes a statement about compulsion and freedom. While the scenes in the plays that we've considered tend to surprise their spectators by emphasising *real* physicality in an otherwise fictional space, by lingering on the treatments of Michael Gove's falling body in the comments on Youtube, we can reflect that it's also often the case that onlookers can choose to reframe a real body as something *unreal* and alien. Though online entities like 'sod-off tax-dodging gits' or 'Tasbo1982' are hardly artists, they nonetheless seek to police the boundaries of the real, presuming to govern the bodies of other people as Shakespeare presumes to govern the bodies of the characters he has created.

Chapter 3

Slosh

According to the *Guinness Book of World Records*, the first throwing of a custard pie on film occurred in *A Noise from the Deep*, a 1913 film featuring Roscoe 'Fatty' Arbuckle and Mabel Normand. The entry goes on to tell us that:

> At first the pies used in slapstick comedies were the real thing, but it was soon found that they had a distressing tendency to disintegrates [sic] in the air. A patisserie called Greenbergs in Glendale, California, came up with a solution to the problem – a special ballistic custard pie with a double thickness of pastry and a filling of flour, water and whipped cream. The filling came in two flavours; blackberry if the recipient was a blonde, lemon meringue for a brunette, to show up better on black and white film.[1]

Using a custard pie as a weapon is now something we think of as a slapstick trope, and indeed the technique of one performer attacking another performer with something fundamentally quite *safe* is a very old one. The term 'slapstick' itself is believed in some quarters to refer to the 'batacchio', a stick wielded in fourteenth-century *commedia dell 'arte* performances by the character Arlecchino (whose name is commonly anglicised as 'Harlequin'). A battachio was constructed with two pieces of wood at one end, so on impact with its victim it would make a sound incommensurate with the pain it would actually cause. That principle — of a violence enacted which sounds or looks worse than it actually is — seems very often to underpin what we might think of as slapstick performance.

In the traditions of physical-comical performance that come

to grow out of *commedia dell 'arte* — in pantomime or in clowning, for example — performers have often attacked one another with buckets of something wet or sticky, a technique that comes to be known more generally as 'slosh'. In her book *Slapstick and Comic Performance: Comedy and Pain,* Louise Peacock finds that such scenes generally consist of the 'relatively harmless throwing of ingredients such as flour and water'.[2] While 'relatively harmless', the ingredients of any given container of slosh reaffirm Alan Dale's summary of the slapstick form:

> often considered the most outrageous of comic styles, and yet, relying as much as it does on such ineluctable forces as gravity, momentum, and bodily functions it's the most necessarily rooted in physical actuality.[3]

As Peacock points out herself, 'the use of "slosh" blurs the boundaries between performance and reality for the audience'.[4] In other words, as outrageous or far-fetched as a performed attack may appear in comparison to the circumstances of 'real life', the performed victim actually gets wet or sticky.

A simple enough act in itself, throwing a custard pie on stage complicates the rules of the dramatic game that we are watching (and, it turns out, participating in). In her history of British pantomime Millie Taylor notes how acts like the throwing of a custard pie create 'a moment of danger and involvement for audiences and performers that increases the awareness of the liveness of each performance'.[5] W. C. Fields was probably being glib when he remarked, 'I never saw anything funny that wasn't terrible,' arguing that, 'if it causes pain, it's funny; if it doesn't, it isn't' — but among those who have written on the subject there seems to be a general agreement that slapstick violence, if it's to be properly entertaining, can neither be considered too real *or* too outlandish.[6] It's in that spirit that Tony Staveacre concludes that slapstick performance is driven along by 'violence — or the parody of violence'.[7] Slosh, then, seems a neat trope by which performers can safely *but recognisably* parody violence. Many of these commentators agree that slapstick enables an onlooker to entertain the possibility that they are witnessing the performance — or perhaps even presence — of 'real pain'. To this end Staveacre's use of *seems* reminds us that the spectator's judgement on this count doesn't just hang upon the content of what they see performed; it depends, too, on *how* it is performed. It's conceivable that a custard pie being thrown at a performer might actually result in some unhappiness on the part of the actor who plays the victim.

Watching such scenes we might claim that we're reassured that nobody is really injured by the fact that the weapon is usually shown to be harmless — a bucket of water, a bucket of flour, a custard pie. But consider these extracts taken from a late-Victorian book called *An Account of Pantomime* and cited by Peacock (and others):

> Toss the baby to *Pantaloon*, crying 'catchee, catchee!' Snatch it away from him, and hit him with it over the shins, knocking him down...Now wash the baby by putting it in a tub, pouring hot water on it from the kettle, and swabbing its face with a mop. Comb its hair with a rake; then put the baby into a mangle and roll it out flat. Set the baby in its cradle, and tread it well down. Make the baby cry; then take it out of bed to quiet it...[8]

This baby is not obviously of the same category as a bucket of slosh; the violence done to it (and with it) is not obviously equivalent to making somebody wet, or sticky or covering them in flour. Violence done to a baby is reprehensible, even taboo; in short, no laughing matter. Clearly, though, these pantomimic episodes were performed in such a way as to align the violence done to the baby with the kind of violence we recognise when we see somebody attacked with slosh. We might think too of Punch and Judy shows, which have traditionally depicted very similar scenes of violence against a baby: here, too, we find that it's the various stylistic factors in the act of performance (rather than the content of the performance, particularly) which reassure us that no real harm is done to the figures in front of us.

When James Pembroke took his son to see *The Bacchae* he observed that 'there were no gasps, no screams, and no requests for post-traumatic counselling'. He wondered in his blog whether the sixth-formers in the audience knew 'better than Cambridge dons that a play is all about pretending'.[9] Of the violent on-stage episodes considered in this chapter so far, even those which haven't depicted some fundamentally *safe* violent action have signalled — by various means — that the violent action is only a *representation* of violent action. In other words, even if we see a baby attacked with a rake rather than a custard pie, when we see it done in pantomime or in a Punch and Judy show we don't worry or get upset: we may even experience the 'satisfaction' that Charles Dickens describes in a letter to a friend about watching a Punch and Judy show, marvelling at 'the circumstance that likenesses of men and women can be so knocked about, without any pain or suffering'.[10] Dickens can watch that Punch and Judy show and know that these are only '*likenesses* of men and women... so knocked about' because they are hand-puppets, and because, as Rosalind Crone notes, they have 'comical and exaggerated features' and wooden faces unable 'to express emotion or pain': this, Crone suggests, means that 'the audience is distanced from the violence and the characters themselves become difficult to identify with'.[11] And many other dominant slapstick traditions rely upon material factors in their staging to 'encourage the audience to view the characters as being removed from reality', as Louise Peacock puts it.[12] She argues, for instance, that when *commedia dell 'arte* is performed, 'the use of half masks diminishes the human connection between performer and audience,' and that in pantomime and clowning cross-dressing and outlandish costume can establish 'an otherness about the performers that mitigates the appearance of pain'.[13]

'Where violence and pain are involved', she goes on, 'in order for the audience to be free to laugh a comic frame must be established.'[14] There are several material factor and performance tropes by which that frame can be put in place, then — but that comic frame isn't always very stable. The wearing of masks or extraordinary costumes, the presence of puppets, the use of pies as a weapon: all of these are concrete and material signals which announce the characters as having been 'removed from reality'. But as we'll see in some of the examples that follow, violence is sometimes performed to such extreme extents that it may serve to remove the performer from an audience's notion of reality even without any obvious recourse to such material signals. How, then, does a spectator interpret a violent action when it suddenly irrupts into a performance where a 'comic frame' hasn't already been obviously established — when an act of violence isn't just committed against the on-stage victim but, conceptually, against the unprepared spectator, too?

Blasted, by Sarah Kane, was first performed in 1995 at the Royal Court Theatre Upstairs. In a review following that first performance (headlined 'This Disgusting Feast of Filth'), the *Daily Mail*'s Jack Tinker described events in the play thus:

> We begin with a journalist indulging in all manner of graphic sexual activity with an underaged and mentally retarded girl in his hotel room somewhere in England. Then we regress, by various implausible stages, from mere unlawful indecency to vividly enacted male rape, through to the barbaric cannibalism of a dead baby and on to simple defecation on stage. [15]

Buying tickets for a 2019 production of the play at RADA,

theatregoers were told that the play 'contains material that some audience members may find challenging', and were invited to view a series of content warnings.[16] But despite what David Greig calls the play's 'litany of broken taboos', and despite the sheer distress the play seems to have been capable of inflicting upon its viewers over the years, several commentators have insisted that an underlying silliness in its composition ought to prevent us taking it seriously.[17] Tinker's eventual conclusion is striking, and rather surprising given the angry tone of the review as a whole: 'Luckily for all of us, the play becomes so risible the only thing to do is laugh.'

Given the play's content it may seem rather odd to wonder how neatly we can fit Louise Peacock's 'comic frame' around it. Yet Kane deploys a range of techniques which would seem to show the characters 'removed from reality'. Where the first two scenes show two characters, Ian and Cate, occupying a hotel room, between the second and third scenes that room is exploded:

Scene Three
The hotel has been blasted by a mortar bomb.
There is a large hole in one of the walls, and everything is covered in dust which is still falling.
The **Soldier** *is unconscious, rifle still in hand.*
He has dropped **Ian**'s *gun which lies between them.*
Ian *lies very still, eyes open.* **(p. 39)**

If this is an extreme and very unexpected development, we might still just about find it consistent with and explained by events in the world of the play (a war is taking place outside the hotel room). As the play progresses, though, it veers still further away from naturalistic staging. After the journalist, Ian, has had his eyes sucked out by the soldier, the presentation of the play grains into a series of vignettes separated by lighting changes:

Darkness.

Light.

Ian *masturbating.*

Ian: cunt cunt cunt cunt cunt cunt cunt cunt cunt cunt cunt

Darkness.

Light.

Ian *shitting.*

And then trying to clean it up with newspaper.

Darkness.

Light.

Ian *laughing hysterically.*

Darkness.

Light.

Ian *having a nightmare.*

Darkness.

Light.

Ian *crying, huge bloody tears.*

He is hugging the Soldier's body for comfort.

Darkness.

Light.

Ian *lying very still, weak with hunger.*

Darkness.

Light.

Ian *tears the cross out of the ground, rips up the floor and lifts the baby's body out.*

He eats the baby.

He puts the remains back in the baby's blanket and puts the bundle back in the hole.

A beat, then he climbs in after it and lies down, head poking out of the floor.

He dies with relief.

It starts to rain on him, coming through the roof.

Eventually.

Ian: Shit. **(pp. 59-60)**

Perhaps not obviously a comic frame, these techniques would seem nevertheless to draw attention to some kind of framing going on. The pattern of the lights fading and rising on a series of new images insist that this is an artificial spectacle, after all, and perhaps, in this respect, the events depicted are meant to be dismissed unproblematically as *not real*. Perhaps the baby eaten here by Ian is meant to be comparable with the pantomime baby bathed in boiling water, combed with a rake, put through a mangle, and thrown about ('catchee, catchee!').

And though most of this content is challenging, even straightforwardly taboo, Kane shows a kind of terse attention to comic timing in her stage directions: noticeable in the repeated '*Darkness./Light.*', and also present in the oddly precise 'Ian shitting' — full stop — 'And then trying to clean it up with a newspaper'; present too, perhaps, in 'He dies with relief' — only then to come back to intone profoundly 'Shit.' Tinker found that the play saw an overall regression 'by various implausible stages' via a series of different atrocities:

> from mere unlawful indecency to vividly enacted male rape, through to the barbaric cannibalism of a dead baby and on to simple defecation on stage.

The formal composition of that regression is important in itself, though: in these closing vignettes the variety of and implausibility of the stages we are witnessing is made increasingly acute. You might think, for instance, that it couldn't get much worse for Ian, *and then it rains*. The contrivance here would seem, again, to frame the whole set up as artificial: still inside, 'head poking out of the floor', he's managed to pick a spot to bury himself where he gets wet when the rain 'comes through the roof'. So even if the content of these vignettes is hardly to be taken lightly, the dramatic patterning and structuring of them seems to have a comic resemblance to it. The content of the play may challenge an audience in its own right, but it also challenges those present to decide how to react: the flippant treatment of atrocity allows little time for serious reflection, and it flirts with the audience's knowledge of comic conventions, inviting laughter while asking if laughter is appropriate or even possible.

As we've seen, not long after *Blasted* was first performed Kane observed that the media had expressed greater outrage about the play than the actual sexual assault of a teenage girl some weeks beforehand. 'The media seems to have been more upset by the representation of violence,' she said, 'than by violence itself.'[18] The nature of the outrage was in itself rather mixed up: reviewing *Blasted* for the *Daily Mail*, Tinker questioned *whether* the play ought to have presented the content that it did, but he also seemed to attack *how* the play presented that content (its 'various implausible stages'). His anxiety about what he deemed a cackhanded or inappropriate artistic approach was nothing new. Shakespeare seasoned *Titus Andronicus* with hundreds of references to artistic forebears, requiring the audience to compare and contrast his representation of atrocity with others like it. In one of the most obvious instances of this, Lavinia — who has been raped, has had her hands cut off and tongue cut out — uses a book about another victim of sexual assault to try and communicate to her father what has been done to her:

Titus: Soft, so busily she turns the leaves.
Help her. What would she find? Lavinia, shall I read?
This is the tragic tale of Philomel,
And treats of Tereus' treason and his rape —
And rape, I fear, was root of thy annoy. **(4.1.41-49)**

As when we're shown Lear cradling Cordelia and invited to think, perhaps, of the *pietà*, Shakespeare invites our critical comparison between artworks — but much more explicitly here, in this, one of his earliest plays. It's notable that none of the characters worry that the comparison might be reductive, or crude; but though it's hard to say for certain whether Shakespeare wants *us* to find the comparison reductive, it's striking that he makes a point of having Lavinia fumble ('Help her'), conspicuously present and conspicuously awkward in a way that exceeds the single point of comparison between her and Philomela.

Like Kane's *Blasted*, Shakespeare's *Titus Andronicus* requires its performers to behave in a ridiculous fashion even as they act out atrocity, distress and trauma. Consider the point at which Shakespeare lingers on the logistical challenges presented to three characters with three hands between them while removing props (two heads and a severed hand) from a stage:

> Come, brother, take a head,
> And in this hand the other will I bear,
> And, Lavinia, thou shalt be employèd in these arms.
> Bear thou my hand, sweet wench, between thy teeth. **(3.1.278-81)**

Earlier, when Lavinia is discovered in a mutilated state by her uncle, Marcus, he laments her misfortune in gorgeous iambic pentameter — going on for 44 lines in total, 'not withstanding all this loss of blood':

> *Enter* **Marcus** *from hunting.*
> **Marcus:** Who is this? My niece that flies away so fast?
> — Cousin, a word. Where is your husband.
> [**Lavinia** *stops and turns.*]
> If I do dream, would all my wealth would wake me;
> If I do wake, some planet strike me down
> That I may slumber an eternal sleep!
> Speak, gentle niece. What stern ungentle hands
> Hath lopped and hewed and made thy body bare
> Of her two branches, those sweet ornaments
> Whose circling shadows kings have sought to sleep in

And might not gain so great a happiness
As half thy love? Why dost not speak to me?
Alas, a crimson river of warm blood,
Like to a bubbling fountain stirred with wind,
Doth rise and fall between thy rosèd lips,
Coming and going with thy honey breath. **(2.4.11-25)**

Not only does the elegance of this verse jar against its grim subject matter, our attention is drawn to a sustained dramaturgical clumsiness: Lavinia's body is not presented in freeze-frame, it is presented as living and moving, breathing and bubbling, rising and falling. Not only is the situation of Marcus inspecting and lamenting his niece's body clearly contrived, the contrivance is highlighted by her frustrated attempt to leave the stage.

Bodies are subjected to slapstick treatment in these plays, then, but crucially they are shown resisting that treatment. By the time Ian eats the dead baby in *Blasted* a spectator may choose to view it as an object rather than a person — as would also likely be the case when watching a baby being battered against the shins of an actor or squeezed through a mangle in the course of a pantomime. But in *Blasted* objectifying the baby takes rather more effort on the part of the spectator: in the scenes prior to this one, Cate has endowed that baby-prop with its own agency and desires, observing, for instance, that it 'keeps crying', and telling Ian 'it's hungry'. In *Titus* Shakespeare shows figures being similarly objectified in how they are presented and described — but, at the same time, he notes how they strain against that objectification. Lavinia is leaving the stage when Marcus prevents her from doing so ('Cousin, a word'). Even as he tries to fix her as a picture— an idyllic composite of branches, circling shadows, a river, a fountain, rosed lips, 'cheeks ...red as Titans face,/Blushing to be encountered with a cloud' — her activity meanwhile reminds us that she is being kept here for his inspection and interpretation. Shakespeare labours the point that, deprived of a tongue, Lavinia cannot speak for herself: 'Shall I speak for thee?' Marcus asks her, speculating about what's been done to her; 'Shall I say 'tis so?' But her thwarted attempt to leave the stage is expressive in itself; the figure of the traumatised victim is not just being spoken for, it is being made to stay where it can be looked at and turned into art.

> Aw. Diddums. Did the nasty fictional play upset you? *Fictional' : Not true. * 'Play' : Not real. **'Travalinman', comment on** *MailOnline*, **'Alas, poor snowflakes', October 2017**

Very few people would mistake either *Blasted* or *Titus Andronicus* for something real. Both plays acknowledge their own artifice fairly frequently, and indeed both plays go to extraordinary lengths to remind their spectators that what's staged is a *representation* of violence. Though neither play has its performers attack one another with custard pies or buckets of water, the violent acts performed in these plays are of such extremity — or performed in such a contrived way — that the spectator understands them as 'a parody of violence' (to return to Tony Staveacre's phrase) rather than actual, physical violence.

But even though these plays prevent their spectators believing the violence depicted to be real, they seek, nevertheless, to upset and discomfit those spectators. The ethics of presenting violence (and interpreting such presentations) is wondered about over and over again in both plays. Consider here, in *Blasted*, for example, when Ian — who earlier raped Cate — has himself been raped by the soldier:

Soldier: You never fucked by a man before?
Ian: (*Doesn't answer.*)
Soldier: Didn't think so. It's nothing. Saw thousands of people packing into trucks like pigs trying to leave town.

Women threw their babies on board hoping someone would look after them. Crushing each other to death. Insides of people's heads came out of their eyes. Saw a child most of his face blown off, young girl I fucked hand up inside her trying to claw my liquid out, starving man eating his dead wife's leg. Gun was born here and won't die. Can't get tragic about your arse. Don't think your Welsh arse is different to any other arse I fucked. Sure you haven't got any more food, I'm fucking starving.

Ian: Are you going to kill me?
Soldier: Always covering your own arse. **(pp. 49-50)**

That bathetic line 'can't get tragic about your arse' is in keeping with the soldier's overall manifesto: there is so much suffering elsewhere, around us, that yours is comparatively insignificant, he argues. The point is grimly playful on Kane's part. Were Ian's suffering as insignificant as the soldier insists, the fact that it's being staged and lingered on would be baffling and gratuitous. But if Ian's suffering is to be afforded consequence, then it feels like it ought to be staged with rather more respect.

Here some features which we'd normally associate with comic performance are co-opted into a presentation that seems callous. The soldier's line 'can't get tragic about your arse' employs an aggressively lowbrow register while accusing his victim of a certain pretentiousness — saying 'tragic' rather than 'traumatised', for instance, accuses Ian of acting things out; that he *gets* tragic implies a certain phoney, perhaps even melodramatic process of performance. Anal rape continues to be couched (and dismissed) in lowbrow, chatty terminology: Ian's 'Welsh arse' is no different, the soldier says, to 'any other arse I fucked'. While these repeated references to Ian's arse associate him with scatology and the body, it's important to note that in many other ways the soldier abstracts it from Ian's possession. The colloquialism 'always covering your own arse' — meaning, broadly, 'always looking to exculpate yourself' — transforms a physical entity ('your Welsh arse') into a figurative site. And even when he refers directly to Ian's body, the soldier's abruptly casual syntax deletes what might otherwise make for an intimate pronoun: 'can't get tragic about your arse' aggressively holds Ian at a distance, where 'you can't get tragic about your arse', 'I can't', or 'people can't' would suggest some possible model for sympathy or understanding even while rejecting it. Kane shows in a phrase like this — applied to a rape— the dispassionate cruelty of a mildly comic performance.

When writing about slapstick violence, some critics have noted its capacity to alter characters' status. In compiling examples of 'slosh' scenes, Millie Taylor found that:

> by far the majority involve the two comics in competition with the lower status comic trying to reverse the roles and wreak comic vengeance on the higher.[19]

Kane embedded similar disparities in status within *Blasted*: 'originally I was writing a play about two people in a hotel room, in which there was a complete power imbalance,' she told Aleks Sierz in an interview for his book *In-yer-face Theatre*, 'which resulted in the older man raping the younger woman'.[20] No matter how little a spectator invests in the 'reality' of the violence depicted on the stage, they might well be troubled by the fact that violence is most often used to consolidate an existing power imbalance rather than challenging it. In Louise Peacock's opinion an onlooker would feel a 'sense of natural justice' when observing a small boy who 'knocks the top hat off a gentleman with a snowball', whereas witnessing 'a child being pelted with snowballs by an adult we are more likely to feel outrage than to be amused'.[21] According to that basic model it doesn't matter that we know the violence perpetrated by Ian against Cate (or by the soldier against Ian) not to be *real*: what it signifies is oppression. And, in that respect, the unnecessariness of the entire performance makes it especially troubling; neither an achievement or even a maintenance of power, but a demonstration of it, gratuitous and sadistic.

Judging a performance of violence to be gratuitous shapes our reading of the power dynamics drawn between a play's characters, then, but it also has important implications for how we understand the power exerted by the writer over the performers, and over us, their spectators. 'Can't get tragic about your arse,' the soldier tells Ian, his victim, and Kane shows us how, in a similarly oppressive way, she prevents her characters from presenting their trauma in a serious way. Talking to Aleks Sierz Kane spoke of:

> nights during rehearsals when I would go home and cry and say to myself: "How could I create that beautiful woman in order for her to be so abused?" And I really did feel a bit sick and depraved.[22]

All writers are responsible for what happens to their characters, of course, but in *Blasted* Kane goes to unusual lengths to acknowledge and draw attention to the authorial treatment of the play's content. Just as we're aware that Shakespeare has the actor playing Lavinia remain on stage to be serially described and spoken for, traipsing around doing ridiculous-looking things, so are we aware that the actor playing Cate in *Blasted* is similarly put up to a series of indignities. Ian bullies Cate throughout the play, but so does Sarah Kane. And you, the spectator: what are you doing? Are you also being bullied by Kane, made to watch this? Or are you joining in with the bullying, laughing at Cate's indignities?

It's an October Thursday in 2016 when I first lecture on this material. Perhaps coincidentally (or perhaps because I'm new)

I've been given a 9am slot. This was the second lecture I've given since I've started this job; the previous week I'd been sure to arrive in plenty of time — to check the PowerPoint worked, to get all the handouts in order — but this week I'd cut it finer. I still had some 10 or 15 minutes before the lecture began when I arrived, but even by the time I started talking — 'right. The *Guinness Book of World Records...*' — I was still slightly out of breath and probably conspicuously unfit and visibly sweating after the cycle from Chesterton, along Chesterton Road, Northampton Street, Madingley Road, Grange Road. The night before I'd bought a ready-made pastry base and a can of squirty cream, and once I'd got the PowerPoint loaded up I filled the base liberally with cream, ready for the lecture. I was an enthusiastic new lecturer, and I was going to use *props*.

I began the lecture and at the appointed time I presented the pie from behind the lectern. When I'd originally conceived of this little gimmick I'd thought I would walk it up and down the stage a little as I read out Millie Taylor's remark that a custard pie such as this one provides 'a moment of danger and involvement for audiences and performers that increases the awareness of the liveness of each performance'. I planned to mention later, too, the review of *Blasted* written by Jane Edwardes for *Time Out*: Kane, she said, 'has proved she can flex her muscles alongside the toughest of men' so now, Edwardes hoped, 'she will learn that repeatedly firing a gun into the audience can only lead to diminishing returns'.[23] What might it mean to attack an audience, I would ask while holding the pie, raising an eyebrow expertly (I imagined), to general laughter and keen interest (I imagined). For whatever reason, though, I stayed behind the lectern: a little embarrassed at how ostentatious a performance that would be, sweaty and out of breath and perhaps more nervous than usual.

In its first form, the lecture moved unannounced from discussing custard pies in performance to discussing how Sarah Kane represented instances of sexual assault in *Blasted*. In first planning out the lecture I'd thought that this move would be a neat way of focussing on the dramaturgical aspects of how these sexual assaults were presented: by comparing the ways in which these scenarios were framed on stage with the throwing of custard pies, I thought, I was making it clear that I was analysing not the *content* of those scenarios so much as their *form*. I knew Kane's play was presenting difficult and potentially upsetting material, but by considering custard pies in performance first I thought I'd be able to signal that we were considering that material in the abstract. Indeed in putting the lecture together I had initially thought to myself (with no little smugness) that the move was unexpected and original. I felt that it was clever: I was pleased with that cleverness. Perhaps, I thought, my students would be slightly wrongfooted by this unexpected move: 'Gosh,' they might think to themselves, 'what a clever man.'

Now, as I delivered the lecture, someone near the back of the lecture hall got up from the bench they were sitting on and slipped out the swing doors at the back of the room. It wasn't obvious if any of the other students in the room had noticed; as I kept talking, though, I began to worry. I had no way of knowing why that student had left. I kept talking. After a few minutes the student came back in and quietly sat down again. Had they nipped out to the toilet? Had a coughing fit driven them out to the corridor? Or had they needed to get out because of what I was talking about and how I was talking about it? In 2013 the Office of National Statistics shared the following figures:

Around one in twenty females (aged 16 to 59) reported being a victim of a most serious sexual offence since the age of 16. Extending this to include other sexual offences such as sexual threats, unwanted touching or indecent exposure, this increased to one in five females reporting being a victim since the age of 16.[24]

At the end of term I noted among the feedback forms some concerns from students who'd attended the lecture. Despite the warnings appended in our *Notes on Courses* document (only one document, after all) one response to the question 'Have you any suggestions as to how the course might be improved if repeated another year?' ran 'content warnings, possibly? *Blasted* pretty awful at 9am'; another was more direct, saying 'It would be good to have a content note on the violence in the *Blasted* seminar, as I wasn't prepared for it.' These responses were marked by understatement, and the first even had something of a gently jokey tone, but it highlighted how conceivable it was — in fact, given the statistics, how it was even rather likely — that there would have been victims of sexual assault among those present in the lecture theatre that day. Furthermore, it was entirely possible that students who had experienced sexual assault didn't feel able to refer to it in a brief scribbled comment on 'how the course might be improved'.

Delivering the lecture the following year, I began it differently: explaining that I'd be talking about custard pies and slosh for a spell, but that I'd then be discussing depictions of sexual assault. I explained my rationale for doing so. Then the lecture carried on much as before: 'right. The *Guinness Book of World Records...*' I've since written elsewhere about my rationale for appending warnings to the lecture in the first place (theguardian.com/commentisfree/2017/oct/31/shakespeare-trigger-warning-students-snowflakes-cambridge-university-sexual-abuse-victims): in sum, the warning had seemed a no-brainer. Why wouldn't I append it? Reports about the lecture's appended warning had shouted that it constituted censorship — but I'd found the warning highly productive, enabling me to talk about material in unexpected ways and drawing unexpected links between challenging content and comic modes of drama.

When I gave the lecture again in 2017 the warning in *Notes on Courses* was not new; it had been there when I first gave the lecture in 2016. While the new preamble in 2017 couldn't really be called censorship, it was intended to change something about the form of the lecture. By announcing the move from custard pies to sexual assault before it was made, I was now hollowing out the 'tada!' element of the 2016 version that I'd been so smug about. Speaking in broad terms, the surprise was pedagogically unnecessary; given the subject matter, it was self-indulgent and crass. More specifically, it was clumsily enacting the power dynamic between performer and audience that I was talking about in both *Blasted* and *Titus Andronicus*. Given what the lecture was about, this wasn't just pointless but perhaps, for some, especially loaded, perhaps especially confrontational. Of *Blasted* and its early critical reception Kane had concluded the following:

> I think the press outrage was due to the play being experiential rather than speculative. The title refers not only to the content but also the impact it seems to have had on audiences. What makes the play experiential is its form.[25]

The notion that the lecture should be at all 'experiential' in the same way was very uncomfortable indeed. Making the comparison between 'slosh' and on-stage rape was one thing, but thinking about the *form* of this discussion highlighted how little value there was in enacting the dramatic phenomena that I was offering for analysis. When Kane and Shakespeare confronted their audiences with abrupt, awkward, even purposefully gratuitous atrocity, the engagement they sought — whatever it might consist of — seemed to be very unlike the kind of engagement my students would find useful when thinking their way through a lecture.

A little less than a year after I'd given my revised lecture: 12 June 2018. The Cambridge University Conservative Association was holding its annual 'Chairman's Dinner', a five-course affair in the Old Kitchens of Trinity College. Their invited speaker, James Delingpole, gave what has been billed as 'an educational talk on Global Political Change'. He later wrote about the talk in his opinion columns for Breitbart and *The Spectator*.

I mentioned the compulsory consent classes you now have to attend as a first-year undergraduate (generally presided over by embarrassed second-years) in which you are lectured on how rape is a bad thing. Then later I made a flippant reference to Jimmy Savile and Rolf Harris. [Non-British readers should know that these were successful children's TV celebrities of the 70s and 80s, later revealed to be predatory sex offenders.][26]

'Several of the alleged "conservatives" at the dinner walked out in protest,' Delingpole observes, speculating that some of the attendees 'might have been plants or entryists who'd gone specifically to be offended so that they could make a political point afterwards'. Among those who left he makes note of a 'visibly distraught girl – escorted by her hissing mate' who, he says, 'called out: "Disgusting!" as she left'. One of Delingpole's 'alleged "conservatives"' later wrote in a column titled 'The CUCA walkout is what political correctness should look like' that 'about a third of the audience' in total left the room over the course of the talk.[27] Nevertheless, Delingpole's write-ups chose instead to make a protagonist of this particular 'visibly distraught' attendee (Breitbart headlined Delingpole's tale 'My Horrible, Horrible Encounter with a "Rape Culture" Cry Bully at Cambridge University').

Two occasions in the same city where a man talks about sexual assault and wonders whether it might be treated in a more or less comic fashion. On each occasion the speaker noted a woman leaving the room. Write about those women in a particular way and they too can be turned into slapstick figures resistant to sympathetic response. When the warning on my

Kane lecture was reported, subsequent opinion columns were notably keen to mock the notional student who might benefit from a prior warning: that mockery tended to place that student at a remove from (and opposed to) reality. David Mitchell's piece in the *Observer* mused that such students 'want to be able to curate their experience of the world to exclude elements they'd rather didn't exist'; A. N. Wilson, in the *Daily Mail*, argued that 'the nice people who want to protect the young from reality are failing to provide them with the tools with which to face that sad thing which the rest of us call life'.[28] This descriptive strategy erects Louise Peacock's 'comic frame' rather neatly: the site of the lecture theatre is not real life, and the people within it are thus not to be thought of as real people. But as *Blasted* and *Titus Andronicus* have shown us, inflicting violence upon the scrutinised figure of a person — if done with stark enough extremity — serves as another way in which a writer can insist that that person ought to be regarded as *not real*. Considering instances where people (not characters) were subjected to such techniques, it's clear that such ad hoc applications of a 'comic frame' are themselves violent; abrupt demonstrations of power over another.

Below James Delingpole's piece for Breitbart, the comments eventually begin to cluster around the 'visibly distraught girl' which he'd described in some detail. Scrolling down you'll encounter the fairly repetitive bugbears of the average Breitbart commenter (people who call themselves 'Freethinker' or 'Red Pilled Thoughtcrimes' and who share exactly the same views as one another): Muslims are rapists and there are too many of them; feminism is ruining everything; liberal men who support feminism are cuckolds; liberals run the world; all of these things — all of them — are a conspiracy. You'll find Delingpole himself responding to some of the comments, helpfully telling us the name of the pub in question; you'll find a spate of comments which appear already to have been deleted (too offensive for

Breitbart?). And sure enough, you'll find 'Mustapha Mond' wishing rape upon the woman who left Delingpole's talk:

> Plonk her in the middle of a muslim area after dark and start the stopwatch. These middle class harpies need a jolt of reality.

Someone called 'John' adds, approvingly, 'she'll see reality when your migrant guests give her the high hard one in the back door.' Tonally these are lines that might have been spoken by one of the rapists in *Blasted*. The woman they are talking about is descriptively transformed into a comic, slapstick body: one plonked and jolted, bumped around but — in terms like these — not, apparently, seriously or lastingly harmed. The colloquial terms that 'John' uses are of a piece with this: not a woman who is raped, but given 'the high hard one'; possessing a body only insomuch that it can be synecdochised and accessed (not a body, but a 'back door').

Slapstick bodies are not commonly *supposed* to arouse our sympathy. As we'll see in the next chapter, the strategies of rendering someone's body a slapstick entity often amount to a concerted artistic or critical refusal to allow that person sympathy when violence is done to them. Doing this is a way of exculpating the viewer from any responsibility for what happens or what has happened to that person. James Delingpole is perfectly open about the fact that he is withdrawing any possibility of sympathy for the woman who left his talk: 'I'd like to stress that I'm not even remotely sorry for any upset I may have caused,' he says in some concluding bullet points, having earlier acknowledged that he caused her significant upset (describing the woman who left his talk as 'visibly distraught'). A feature of comic performance is applied to a real-life victim: this person, the writer insists, is of no real consequence.

Among the comments posted underneath Delingpole's

article, those from 'Mustapha Mond' and 'John' are part of a general trend towards dehumanising minority groups and vulnerable people. In such company, their tone isn't, perhaps, all that noteworthy: their intentions are to demean someone, and refusing to take that person seriously is a way of doing that. But as well as demeaning them, the strategies of turning someone into a slapstick body also, importantly, render that person as an entity who is incapable of receiving sympathy. In the moment of their getting up and leaving the room, they can be presentationally transformed into bodies alien and unlike our own. Just like RSC insiders who term passed-out audience members 'droppers', the people calling themselves 'Mustapha Mond' and 'John' on Breitbart seek to redesignate a person as an object susceptible to physics but not emotions. Theirs, they say with their tone, is a *parody* of violence; the victim — they insist — does not feel 'real pain', because the victim, they imply, *cannot* feel 'real pain'.

Chapter 4

No Two Alike

In the years before they made it big in the movies, the Marx Brothers occasionally exploited their strong physical resemblance to one another by swapping roles during performances — sometimes, it seems, just for the hell of it. In his biography of Groucho, Stefan Kanfer describes how, in the final week of *The Cocoanuts* running on Broadway, Harpo and Chico 'changed places onstage, wearing each other's wigs and doing each other's shtick'; 'not a soul in the audience', Kanfer tells us, 'could tell the difference'.[1] In their youth, the two eldest brothers had played a similar trick: Chico took on so much work playing the piano in New York honky-tonk bars that he was forced to enlist as a surrogate 'his lookalike, Adolph [i.e. Harpo], who had picked up what little keyboard technique he knew from his elder brother'.[2] Consider, too, the story printed in the Chicago *American* in October 1930, which revealed to anybody attending the Marx Brothers' latest production that the 'Groucho' on-stage was not, in fact, Groucho:

> The man with the big black moustache was in fact Zeppo, who had stepped in for his brother. Groucho could be found in a bed at the Michael Reese hospital, where he was recovering from an emergency appendectomy.[3]

In such accounts as these, the Marx Brothers are rendered simply and instantly distinguishable by their particular effects (by 'each other's wigs' or 'each other's schtick' or a 'big black moustache', or similar) — and, at the same time, they are shown to be radically and unusually interchangeable. In these instances, such a state of affairs is usually presented as consistent with the

Marx Brothers' brand of comedy: anarchic and rather mad.

The brothers' most famous exploration of their shared resemblance was staged in their 1936 film *Duck Soup*. Disguised as Groucho's character (Rufus T. Firefly), Chico (Ravelli) and Harpo (Pinky) undertake to steal his military plans. Rumbled, Pinky seeks to escape; he runs full pelt into a mirror, which smashes. Once Firefly catches up, Pinky pretends to be his reflection, mimicking his movements with increasing inaccuracy. Eventually Ravelli wanders into the frame of the 'mirror', and the illusion of reflection is finally irrevocably ruined. Thinking again of Bergson's theories of comedy we might reflect that these mirror scenes are straightforward exhibitions of mechanistic movement; of humans as automatons. When Groucho moves, Harpo must mimic the movement compulsively. As the scene progresses, the reflection is all that matters: volition is abandoned on either side of the imagined 'glass' as Groucho moves more and more unpredictably to try and catch Harpo out. And then, even as this scene threatens to attain a kind of grace, both characters begin to bumble; their movements strive to fit a pattern and fail; both robbed of thought, but neither achieving the geometry of a true reflection. Writing about the scene in the *Financial Times* in 2015, Danny Leigh said it gives rise to 'the kind of ecstatic comedy in which the world outside the cinema simply falls away'.[4] The Marx Brothers succeed, it seems, in establishing a particularly successful 'comic frame': not only signalling clearly the unreal aspects of the performance, but — if Leigh is correct — helping the spectator escape from the 'real' world.

This mirroring 'bit' had a rich slapstick heritage, itself mirroring, as critics like Tony Staveacre have pointed out, countless precedents in vaudeville and pantomime. Staveacre lists versions of the mirror scene which he has found in a vaudevillian's diary entry in 1911, in an account of performances at the Cirque Olympique in 1848, in accounts of performances in New York in 1860, and in a Harlequinade at Drury Lane in the late nineteenth century.[5] We can also note with Staveacre many film and television treatments of the mirror scene subsequent to *Duck Soup*: Abbott and Costello have a go; a 'mirror scene' features in the *Tom and Jerry* episode 'Cat and Dupli-cat'; Harpo Marx revisits the scene in an episode of *I Love Lucy* with Lucille Ball; Woody Allen includes a version in his 1973 film *Sleeper*; in 2014, the Muppets incorporate a mirror scene in *Muppets Most Wanted*. These mirror scenes explore the phenomenon of bodily automatism in the course of their being performed, but they're so much a trope in themselves that most performers (and spectators) recognise that an actor's own volition is also of secondary importance to the overall demands of the scenario. In her history of British pantomime, Millie Taylor notes a script for a 1991 production of *Mother Goose* which 'simply announces that "Billy and Mother Goose do the mirror routine plus dance at end"'.[6] Indeed Taylor points out that only one rehearsal of the scene was considered necessary by the performers in that production; she records the deputy stage manager's 'astonishment that the accuracy and timing were so precise given that the routine had not been performed for nearly a year'.[7] Thus individual volition — whether we think of it as the character's or the *actor's* — is subsumed into the requirements of the overall scene.

More generally, and outside the specific demands of the 'mirror scene', there is a rich tradition of performers mining the confusion which arises from physical resemblance to achieve straightforwardly comic effects. And when we consider other works which linger on the phenomenon of physical resemblance, it's striking that over-emphasising characters' physical likeness is normally one way to reassure us that we're not supposed to worry about a particular individual's welfare as we watch bad things happening to them. *One Man, Two Guvnors*, first staged at the National Theatre in 2011 and touring on and off since then, is routinely and unproblematically advertised as a comedy: take, for instance, the *Telegraph*'s assertion that it constitutes 'comic perfection' or the *Guardian* celebrating its 'triumph of visual and verbal comedy'.[8] Charles Spencer, writing for the *Telegraph*, was quoted prominently on the play's posters, saying it was 'one of the most hilarious shows I have ever seen in a theatre'.[9] Packed full of exaggerated violence, physical mishaps and a great many other bits of slapstick business, the storyline for *One Man, Two Guvnors* rests upon a single man struggling to play out the functions of two, and it features a sister disguised as (and unproblematically mistaken for) her dead brother. The storyline is an adaptation of Carlo Goldoni's 1743 *A Servant for Two Masters*, which itself draws heavily on earlier *commedia dell 'arte* tropes of mistaken and switchable likenesses. These plays are part of a long and somewhat familiar theatrical tradition, in which interchangeable personhood is normally equated with comic effect. We might consider, for example, that some 1800 years earlier than Goldoni, the Roman dramatist Plautus was presenting a series of scenarios where the twins Menaechmus of Epidamnus and Menaechmus of Syracuse are mistaken for one another, in his play *Menaechmi*; *this* play was very likely a source for Shakespeare's *Comedy of Errors*, which shows not one but two sets of twins serially mixed up. Like *One Man, Two Guvnors* and *A Servant for Two Masters*, the *Menaechmi* and *The Comedy of Errors* are mostly regarded as funny, unworrisome pieces of drama, despite the characters frequently being subjected to physical violence. Indeed in its online archive, the Royal Shakespeare Company glosses all of the productions of *The Comedy of Errors* staged between 1938 and the present day as versions of what it terms, simply enough, a 'farcical comedy of twins and mistaken identity'.[10] In all the productions of all these plays, the point at which individual identity becomes interchangeable — something that can be mistaken, or swapped — is taken to suggest that all events that befall the individual are to be understood as amusing. That interchangeability is also, in itself, offered primarily as a source of amusement rather than concern.

Why is 'mistaken identity' so often bound up with the effects of 'farcical comedy'? Perhaps it owes something to the fact that plays of confusing likeness — like *The Comedy of Errors*, or *One Man, Two Guvnors* — are stocked with especially blatant signals that all of what's presented is simple dramatic pretence, not to be taken seriously. Of the RSC productions of *The Comedy of Errors* to have been mounted since 1938, for instance, no Antipholuses or Dromios have been acted by identical twins (Ian Judge's 1990 production used one actor apiece for both Antipholuses and both Dromios, utilising doubles only at the play's conclusion when all four twins appear on stage at the same time — a moment which even the RSC admits 'felt unsatisfying since, all along, the play has been assiduously whetting the audience's appetite to see the full set of brothers meet at last'.[11]) By far the majority of productions of the play have attached easy, visual signals of likeness to their actors: in Adrian Noble's 1983 version the Antipholuses 'dressed alike' and 'both had blue faces' while the Dromios 'had garish check suits, clown faces and red noses'; in Theodor Komisarjevsky's 1938 production, 'bowler hats of different colours' were used. As a result — much like the Marx Brothers — the figures of both Antipholuses and both Dromios have normally been understood as avatars rather than people, merely a set of readily distinguishable (and easily transferable) physical features. When figures are seen to be this much like each other, we don't worry too much about what happens to any single individual within that group. As with some of the material factors of performance noted by Rosalind Crone and Louise Peacock and considered in the previous chapter, these are means by which we might recognise the figures before us to exist only within a 'comic frame'.

When my lectures' warnings were reported in 2017, my students were also rendered more or less interchangeable with one another, and so framed as fundamentally comic figures. 'Famous Plays come with Trigger Warnings at Cambridge

University', the headline in *Newsweek* told its readers, posing the question 'Shakespeare for Snowflakes?' 'Alas,' the *Daily Mail* intoned in its equivalent headline, 'poor snowflakes!' The tag was taken up enthusiastically in scores of online comments.

> not surprised by these pathetic spineless snowflakes who want everything on a plate but moan and complain when it doesn't go their way #offended snowflakes[12]

Whether on Breitbart's comment threads, or the *Daily Mail*'s website, or even on the local website *Cambridgeshire Live*, the students were frequently referred to *en masse* as snowflakes. This was a simple enough process of stereotyping, of course. But by using this chapter to examine the specific ways in which 'snowflakes' are modelled, I hope to show that the presentational strategies used to transform a given person into a 'snowflake' — denying them a subjective, individual experience — greatly resemble the particular means by which slapstick figures in theatre are also rendered as assortments of visible and easily interchangeable features. Endowing a person with such traits is one way in which a spectator can be relieved of the anxieties that might otherwise arise from wondering whether to sympathise with that person, or through worrying about *how* to sympathise with them. And — as we'll see — this process isn't just enacted in the theatre, and it isn't just enacted by writers on the spectators' behalf: often enough it's enacted by the spectators themselves, while regarding events which are not fictitious, in media which are not obviously theatrical, concerning people who are not willingly presenting themselves as characters.

In responding to the stories about the warnings appended to my lectures, most of the people who made comment-thread allegations of snowflakery presumably did so in passing. Inasmuch as that might be the case, my claiming that snowflakes are *modelled* in a particular way — talking of *presentational strategies,* and such — may sound overly grand, presenting the commenters' undertaking (perhaps illegitimately, perhaps even, in some cases, ludicrously) as an act of deliberative, thoughtful craft. But such comments were part of a wider discourse which extends into forms which are more obviously thought through and more obviously designed to be exhibited to a wide readership. Take the example of an article written by Greg Lukianoff and Jonathan Haidt, published by *The Atlantic* in 2015 and given the title 'The Coddling of the American Mind': an extended argument against what the writers call 'a movement' among university staff and students which is effecting 'to scrub campuses clean of words, ideas, and subjects that might cause discomfort or give offense'.[13] For Lukianoff and Haidt, attending to possible microaggressions and thinking about (and providing) trigger warnings leads to an overall culture of what they termed 'vindictive protectiveness'. They believe that within this culture students are encouraged 'to develop extra-thin skin in the years just before they leave the cocoon of adult protection and enter the workforce'. Though the article was careful not to use the term 'snowflake', by arguing that the 'movement' that they were describing 'presumes an extraordinary fragility of the collegiate psyche', they lent a touch of scholarly polish to some of the attitudes seen in many comment-thread discussions of snowflakery. According to *The Atlantic*'s editor, the article generated a 'tidal wave of reaction'.[14] Indeed in the past 3 years it has already been cited in more than 200 different academic articles and monographs, and in their later book on the subject — also called *The Coddling of the American Mind* — Lukianoff and Haidt were keen to stress the initial article's overall reach while talking up its influence: it became, they point out, 'one of the five most-viewed articles of all time on *The Atlantic*'s website, and President Obama even referred to it in a speech a few weeks later'.[15] Whether their work was as influential as they claim or whether it codified anxieties which were already doing the rounds, their publications serve as particularly useful touchstones for how 'snowflakes' can be identified, and they offer a particular set of theories about how such 'snowflakes' are constructed.

The culture that Lukianoff and Haidt make out and name 'vindictive protectiveness' — what's elsewhere termed 'snowflake culture' — is founded on two elements. First, in the view set out by Lukianoff and Haidt, the subjective experience of the individual — how that person feels — has been given undue weight in everyday campus discourse and behaviour: an unhelpful privileging of 'emotional reasoning', they argue. Second, they believe that university students and staff are too much engaged in anticipating how other people might feel. They posit that trigger warnings and concerns about microaggressions arise from the mistaken belief 'that exposure to the hateful thing could traumatize some *other* people. You believe that you know how others will react, and that their reaction could be devastating.'[16] Though they're not obviously likening university students to the Marx Brothers, they do describe empathic processes in a way that stages them within a crazy sort of mirror scene. By situating online comments alongside more academic work like Lukianoff and Haidt's, this chapter will note how often the action of calling a person a snowflake is posed as a wider political or sociological argument like Lukianoff and Haidt's — but it will also show how work like Lukianoff and Haidt's seeks to stage a drama which has a form very like that written out in online comments.

Calling a person a snowflake is to insist on a particular empathic relationship between any onlookers and the person under scrutiny. Whether discussed in terms infused with academic flavours ('vindictive protectiveness') or in the blunt and sometimes aggressive language of online comment threads ('snowflakery'), the performance of empathy between people often comes to be reframed as something facile and mechanical, akin to Harpo dressing in Groucho's clothes and mimicking his movements. Calling someone a snowflake is like any other process of stereotyping in very many respects, of course, but it also has an unusual utility for turning that person into a particular kind of figure: so ruled by 'feeling', so tuned to anticipating the feelings of others that their actions are ridiculous, automatic, arbitrary. In the discussions which we'll be examining in this chapter, anyone who thinks they anticipate the feelings of another, who conditions their words and behaviour accordingly, is rendered as ludicrous as either figure in a mirror scene. To fully transform these sympathising figures from figures that we might ourselves empathise with into figures that we don't *need* to empathise with, it's necessary to portray their sympathising relationship as a childish, slapstick kind of mirroring. By doing this, an individual's experience of the world is effaced: they are re-presented as a composite of external traits — not wigs, glasses and greasepaint moustaches, of course, but behaviours.

The pertinent definition for 'snowflake' in the *Oxford English Dictionary* underscores how the term actively hollows out the person we apply it to. 'Snowflake', we're told, referred 'originally' to 'a person, esp. a child, regarded as having a unique personality and potential', but 'later' to 'a person mockingly characterized as overly sensitive or easily offended'.[17] The identification and mockery of snowflakes relies, then, on somehow recognising (from the outside) that the 'snowflake' in question considers their individual experience of the world to be individual to them, while also insisting (from the same vantage point) that this is not the case. 'That person thinks they're unique — but they're not.'

Telling upset people that they're not unique is a venerable tradition. When the grieving Hamlet concedes that it's common to lose a loved one, his mother, Gertrude, asks: 'If it be/Why seems it so particular with thee?' (1.2.74-5) And though it was Hamlet's uncle and now step-father Claudius who murdered

Hamlet's father, he doesn't let that stop him issuing a rough-and-ready 'pull yourself together':

> 'Tis sweet and commendable in your nature, Hamlet,
> To give these mourning duties to your father,
> But you must know your father lost a father,
> That father lost, lost his...**(1.2.87-90)**

And 'To persever/In obstinate condolement' like this, Claudius tells us, is consistent with 'unmanly grief', 'a heart unfortified', and 'a mind impatient,/An understanding simple and unschooled' (92-7). As if to underline the message that "tis common' to experience the grief that Hamlet is experiencing, Shakespeare plants other unfathered sons as mirrors to Hamlet through the rest of the play — see, for example, the Norwegian prince Fortinbras, named, like Hamlet, after his father, or Laertes, who loses his father Polonius to Hamlet's sword. Indeed Hamlet himself participates in a society which insists roughly and rudely that no one person can have a monopoly on grief. Here, for example, he pits his grief against that of Laertes, who is mourning his sister, Ophelia:

> Forty thousand brothers
> Could not with all their quantity of love
> Make up my sum.

'An thou'lt mouth,' Hamlet says, 'I'll rant as well as thou' (5.2.248-50; 262-3). While Hamlet and Laertes jostle with one another to see who grieves Ophelia's death the most, we may recall the argument made by the soldier to Ian in *Blasted* after listing the atrocities of war: there's so much suffering experienced by everyone, the soldier says, 'can't get tragic about your arse'.

But over the centuries, readers have tended to note and to celebrate Hamlet's singularity. 'Tis not alone my inky cloak...

that can denote me truly,' he tells his mother, claiming: 'I have that within/Which passes show' (1.2.77; 83; 85). In saying so, though, he's not necessarily making a claim to be an enigmatic and fascinating person; he is, in the first instance, responding to this injunction from his mother:

> Good Hamlet, cast thy nighted colour off
> And let thine eye look like a friend on Denmark.
> Do not forever with thy veilèd lids
> Seek for thy noble father in the dust— **(1.2.68-71)**

A person's trauma might not be immediately obvious to an onlooker; this is something that most people would think themselves ready enough to accept, and indeed it's a feature of accounts of trauma which we might even find culturally quite familiar. Google the fairly hackneyed journalistic phrases 'withdrew into himself' or 'withdrew into herself' and you'll find stories of mothers grieving for lost sons, of victims of molestation and sexual assault, of people confronted with life-changing medical diagnoses or subjected to chronic pain conditions. In *Trauma and Recovery*, a study hailed since publication as 'a landmark' and 'one of the most important psychiatric works to be published since Freud', Judith Herman observes that: 'Traumatic events have primary effects not only on the psychological structures of the self but also on the systems of attachment and meaning that link individual and community.'[18] Going on, she quotes a rape survivor whose account recalled 'how the trauma disrupted her sense of connection with others': 'there's no way to describe what was going on inside me...I felt as if my whole world had been kicked out from under me and I had been left to drift alone in the darkness'.[19] Herman begins *Trauma and Recovery* with these lines:

The ordinary response to atrocities is to banish them from

consciousness. Certain violations of the social compact are too terrible to utter aloud: this is the meaning of the word *unspeakable*.[20]

This, it seems, leads to the feeling of drifting alone in the darkness: unable to utter his or her experience of atrocity (or perhaps not allowed to do so), the traumatised individual must find a way, as Herman puts it, 'to restore her sense of connection with the wider community'.[21] The widespread use of that formulation 'withdrew into himself/herself' shows how readily our community has turned the individual disconnected by trauma into something of a trope.

Herman's opening lines are carefully and interestingly reflexive: *who* banishes atrocity, we might ask, and from *whose* consciousness? *Who* decides that a violation is 'too terrible' to be named and talked about? Those first lines are, perhaps, designed to draw attention to the role of the spectator in the traumatised individual's experience of trauma. In that chapter on 'Disconnection' Herman goes on to refer to an article written by Alice Sebold and published in the *New York Times* in 1989 under the headline 'HERS; Speaking the Unspeakable', a piece in which Sebold recounted her own sexual assault and spoke of the events that followed it. In a later memoir, *Lucky*, Sebold remembers her walk home immediately after being raped:

I was aware I was being stared at...They talked. But I wasn't there. I heard them outside of me, but like a stroke victim, I was locked inside my body.[22]

This account highlights in immediate terms the 'disconnection' that Herman outlines and reflects on in *Trauma and Recovery*. But, despite the literary and cultural conventions by which we allow a victim of trauma to have 'that within which passeth show', to occupy a position 'inside' their own bodies, accounts and presentations of such trauma also often show an external gaze working in counterpoint to the traumatised individual's experience. Sebold recalled in her *New York Times* article how, while waiting for the police to arrive following the rape, 'my fellow students stared at me as if I were a girl on a TV screen' and how 'in the following years, throughout the trial, which ended in 1982, many remained unable to do more than stare'.[23] Importantly, that gaze often seems to regard the traumatised individual's experience with a certain scepticism. In *Lucky*, Sebold herself recounts how, learning of a classmate's own sexual assault some months later, she remarked to a friend that, unlike her, 'she'll wear the rape eternally'; 'Cast thy nighted colour off,' Gertrude tells her Hamlet.[24] In such formulations as these, trauma is described as being worn by the victim and seen from the outside.

Such instances might just rest as writers acknowledging the difficulties encountered in trying to know what somebody else is going through when they have been traumatised. But very often those difficulties appear to lead to an onlooker doubting (or even denying outright) the individuality of a trauma victim's experience of the world. Lukianoff and Haidt express their firm opinion that efforts to second-guess that person's experience are taken too far and too often by too many people.

> Grossly expanded conceptions of trauma are now used to justify the overprotection of children of all ages — even college students, who are sometimes said to need safe spaces and trigger warnings lest words and ideas put them in danger.[25]

Their scepticism is ostensibly directed at the onlooker's response; talking of 'grossly expanded conceptions of trauma' and of 'overprotection' seems not to argue against the possibility of trauma existing, but argues instead that we too often mistake someone's non-traumatic discomfort for the kind of trauma which Lukianoff and Haidt would consider authentic. But, like Gertrude telling her son to 'cast [his] nighted colour off', Lukianoff and Haidt emphasise that their viewpoint is removed from the victim, and that the victim is to be considered from the outside. Even when they concede that 'for a student who truly suffers from PTSD [post-traumatic stress disorder], appropriate treatment is necessary', their 'truly' betrays their mistrust: how can we know that the traumatised behaviours we witness in another person correspond to an authentic experience of trauma?

In noting how the *Diagnostic and Statistical Manual of Mental Disorders* definition of 'trauma' has morphed over the years (and become, they say, 'grossly expanded'), Lukianoff and Haidt stumble on a problem inherent to communicating and understanding trauma.

the criteria for a traumatic event that warrants a diagnosis of PTSD were (and are) strict: to qualify, an event would have to 'evoke significant symptoms of distress in almost everyone' and be 'outside the range of usual human experience'. The DSM III emphasized that the event was not based on a *subjective standard*. It had to be something that would cause most people to have a severe reaction.

Lukianoff and Haidt complain that 'by the early 2000s...The *subjective experience* of "harm" became definitional in assessing trauma.'[26] But we can see that some 2 decades earlier the *DSM* III was already struggling to talk around the kind of subjective experience that determines a traumatic event to be traumatic. How, in short, do we identify an event that would likely 'evoke significant symptoms of distress in almost everyone' *if* that event is 'outside the range of usual human experience'?

It's difficult to undertake the imaginative or empathic leap required to try and put yourself in the place of someone who has undergone an experience that is particular to them and, in that sense, alien to you. This is especially the case when the experience does not seem to have any shared, external reference points. Lukianoff and Haidt point out that psychological trauma was initially understood as having a physical cause:

> In the early versions of the primary manual of psychiatry, the *Diagnostic and Statistical Manual of Mental Disorders* (DSM), psychiatrists used the word 'trauma' only to describe a physical agent causing physical damage, as in the case of what we now call *traumatic brain injury*. In the 1980 revision, however, the manual (DSM III) recognized 'post-traumatic stress disorder' as a mental disorder—the first type of traumatic injury that isn't physical.[27]

In the context of the previous chapters' discussions of bodies being rendered slapstick in performance, it's notable how an individual suffering from post-traumatic stress disorder occupies a body which appears especially inscrutable when compared with a body which is subjected to physical trauma. Inasmuch as it might manifest with physical behaviours at all, PTSD is a condition which transforms the sufferer's body into something which — to an observer — appears to be composed of arbitrary and inexplicable actions. And, by describing that person from an emphatically distanced and external viewpoint, a writer can diminish or dismiss outright the importance of any non-physical ailments that might be afflicting that person. Not only that, and as we have seen in previous chapters, describing a figure as if from such a viewpoint tends to confine that person within a body which is only considered a physical entity, and thus within a set of artistic traditions which we associate with slapstick and with comedy more generally.

When the novelist Siri Hustvedt began shaking uncontrollably while delivering a talk at St Olaf's College, Minnesota, in honour of her dead father, it appeared to onlookers 'that some unknown force had suddenly taken over' Hustvedt's body and administered 'a good, sustained jolting'.[28] In the years that followed, Hustvedt tried to identify the cause for this pathological shaking, a process she sets out in her book, *The Shaking Woman, Or, A History of My Nerves*. Consulting specialists in a range of different medical fields —travelling 'in the worlds of neurology, psychiatry, and psychoanalysis', as she puts it — leads her to no obvious conclusion; nor, after years of multiple treatments and diagnoses, is Hustvedt able to conclude whether her pathology has arisen due to circumstances in her neurological state or her psychological being.[29] 'I now have a psychoanalyst-psychiatrist and a neurologist treating me, but neither of them can tell me who the shaking woman is,' Hustvedt reflects.[30] The different ways of looking at her and her relationship with her body's shaking can easily fall into opposition, she points out, referring to a widely shared and discussed *New York Times* headline, 'Is Hysteria Real?', which, she says, 'upholds the conventional belief: if you can see it, it's real and physical. If you can't, it's unreal and mental.'[31]

Hustvedt's is at first a discussion of different medical approaches to her own particular affliction, but it's also an invitation to reflect on how we choose to describe the experience of a given person who is not us. In unpicking the reductive oppositions between neurology and psychiatry, the bodily and the mental, she observes that 'the philosophical ideas that lie beneath calling one thing by one name and another by another often remain unexamined, and they may be determined more by intellectual fashions than by rigorous thought'.[32] This pertains primarily to the wider trends that may govern the reading of a particular phenomenon: do we interpret it as something mental, or physical? Are we considering a mind, or a brain? But Hustvedt's conclusions also challenge us to think through the decisions that often drive the ways in which other people are *written*. In this light, a text like Lukianoff and Haidt's *Coddling of the American Mind* is not just a thesis but a kind of theatre, choosing to present people from particular angles, figuring them in particular ways, making them out of particular stuff. Hustvedt's is a different kind of theatre again, written in such a way that the figure who is described we imagine is one capable of an inner life, even if that inner life remains ultimately obscured to and removed from us.

Among Lukianoff and Haidt's various anxieties about the culture of 'vindictive protectiveness' which they say is prevalent on university campuses today, chief is their worry that a series of 'cognitive distortions' are taking hold of young people, and that those distortions are indulged and even consolidated by current pedagogical practice. Their original article for *The Atlantic* appended a compressed list of 'nine of the most common cognitive distortions that people learn to recognize in CBT [cognitive behavioural therapy]', which they took from a single source, *Treatment Plans and Interventions for Depression and Anxiety Disorders*. A version of this list, expanded to a page, also appeared in their later book. Because the understanding of what constitutes trauma has been 'grossly expanded', in their view, and because 'the *subjective experience* of "harm" became definitional in assessing trauma', they consider it especially necessary to correct the errant subjectivities which underpin any given 'cognitive distortion'. But the apparent valorisation of objectivity throughout Lukianoff and Haidt's work is in fact an affirmation of a carefully constructed (and limited) viewpoint. Consider again their complaint that:

> The DSM III emphasized that the [traumatic] event was not based on a *subjective standard*. It had to be something that would cause most people to have a severe reaction.

As Siri Hustvedt points out — and as we might deduce from its title — this *Diagnostic and Statistical Manual* 'is purely descriptive', intended 'to collect symptoms under headings that will help a physician diagnose patients'.[33] In iterating and reiterating lists of symptoms, Lukianoff and Haidt are having their reader inhabit not the sufferer's experience but the physician's gaze, regarding the figure of the sufferer from a detached distance.

As readers we may be habituated to construing such features as conventions of objectivity: the physician's gaze being equivalent to something like proper critical detachment. But Hustvedt reminds us of an important corollary to that external gaze: the inhabited experience.

> The *DSM* does not tell stories. It contains no cases of actual patients or even fictional ones. Etiology, the study of the *cause* of illness, isn't part of the volume. Its mission is purely descriptive, to collect symptoms under headings that will help a physician diagnose patients... The fact is that all patients have stories, and those stories are necessarily part of the *meaning* of their illnesses.[34]

In Hamlet's everyday world, it would seem that he feels very few of the people around him allow him his own singular story. He is, we are told at one point, 'th'observed of all observers', over and over again looked at, questioned and talked about. This explains in part, perhaps, his rather plaintive request to Horatio as he lies dying: 'tell my story' (5.2.327). Yet even if Hamlet notes correctly that most in the court do not allow him the singularity of *his* grief ('That father lost, lost his'; 'Why seems it so particular with thee?'), the playwright, at least, *does* afford him a great deal of singularity in the way he is presented. Hamlet speaks more lines by far than any other character (more than any other character in a single play across Shakespeare's entire canon, in fact), and a great many of those lines are spoken uninterrupted as monologues and soliloquies. And, although Gertrude may ask him to 'cast off' his black clothes in the first scene in which he appears, the very fact that he's dressed like this acts to distinguish him by stark, visual means from all other figures on the stage. Even if the precise motivations of the character Hamlet may prove recurrently and naggingly inscrutable to the audience, by these measures and many others the play *Hamlet* does try to tell his story over and above anyone else's.

Other plays come closer to modelling people as Lukianoff and Haidt do in their writings on 'vindictive protectiveness'. For all that *The Comedy of Errors* showcases many traits that enable us to accept it easily enough as, say, a 'farcical comedy of twins and mistaken identity', Shakespeare embeds occasional suggestions that experiencing one's identity as interchangeable is profoundly stressful. Thought to be mad based on his twin's behaviour around the town, Antipholus of Ephesus is subjected to the ministrations of a certain Dr Pinch:

> They brought one Pinch, a hungry, lean-faced villain;
> A mere anatomy, a mountebank,
> A threadbare juggler, and a fortune-teller,
> A needy, hollow-eyed, sharp-looking wretch,
> A living dead man. This pernicious slave
> Forsooth took on him as a conjurer,
> And gazing in mine eyes, feeling my pulse,
> And with no face, as 'twere, outfacing me,
> Cries out I was possessed. **(5.1.237-45)**

The therapy administered by Pinch and his attendants is disturbing in itself: Antipholus is bound and borne to 'a dark and dankish vault' and left there until, he says, 'gnawing with my teeth my bonds in sunder', he escapes. But, more disturbing still, the image of Antipholus being outfaced by a figure with *no* face signals the culmination of his losing a sense of unique, individual identity. In the course of the play, Antipholus of Ephesus has been rendered itinerant from the visual signifiers normally used to identify him, to the extent that he now describes a situation where he is mirrored by a void.

It's possible that Shakespeare was trying to write a 'farcical comedy of mistaken identity' and somehow ended up larding his characters' speeches with psychologically interesting turns of phrase — if he'd written for the Marx Brothers perhaps he wouldn't have been able to stop himself interposing a monologue about what it means to be *human* somewhere in the mirror scene. It's not obviously *funny* when Antipholus of Syracuse says the following about finding his twin brother, for example:

> I to the world am like a drop of water
> That in the ocean seeks another drop,
> Who, falling there to find his fellow forth,
> Unseen, inquisitive, confounds himself. **(1.2.35-8)**

But this isn't an isolated point of anxiety: *The Comedy of Errors* is animated throughout by an ongoing concern that characters are losing control of what makes them *them,* long before Dr Pinch is brought onto the stage to outface Antipholus of Ephesus with a void. At all turns characters wonder obsessively if those around them are going mad: 'Why, mistress, sure my master is horn mad', Dromio of Ephesus reasons (2.1.57); 'wast thou mad', Antipholus of Ephesus asks Dromio of Syracuse, 'that this so madly thou didst answer me?' (2.2.11-2); Luciana, wife of Antipholus of Ephesus, speaking to Antipholus of Syracuse and mistaking him for her husband, asks: 'What, are you mad, that you do reason so?' (3.2.53) Dispossession of the self is the kind of serious matter that Shakespeare treats with more proper gravity elsewhere: think of Lear worrying to himself 'let me not be mad' after he has given away his kingdom and apparently lost the love of his daughters; 'not mad. Sweet heaven,' he says, 'keep me in temper; I would not be mad' (2.139-41). But in an earlier play like *The Comedy of Errors* Shakespeare may have been exploring the ways in which dispossessing someone of their individuality in a flippant, comic mode can particularly compound their loss and their powerlessness. Perhaps that features in *Lear* too, albeit rather more succinctly, when Lear asks a gaggle of bystanders 'who is't can tell me who I am?' and the Fool replies: 'Lear's shadow' (1.4.199-200).

Reading Alice Sebold's account of events in *Lucky*, it's remarkable how often she was physically scrutinised in the months following her rape; perhaps accordingly her memoir draws attention to the instances in which narratives were constructed and laid upon her based on her physical appearance. The procedures of investigating the rape and prosecuting the rapist demand that Sebold is herself looked at and itemised. In giving an initial statement to the police, for example, she is told (often angrily): 'That's inconsequential, just the facts.'

> I took each reprimand for what it was: an awareness that the specificity of my rape did not matter, but only how and if it conformed to an established charge. Rape 1, Sodomy 1, etc. How he twisted my breasts or shoved his fist up inside me, my virginity: inconsequential.[35]

Later she is acutely conscious of how she will be looked at in the courtroom. She details the process of clothes shopping in preparation for her appearance before the rapist (Gregory Madison), a judge, and a jury, and she describes her entrance to the courtroom in these terms:

> I was frightened and shaking when I crossed the courtroom, passed the defense table, the judge at the podium, the prosecution table, and came to take the stand. I liked to think I was Madison's worst nightmare, although he didn't know it yet. I represented an eighteen-year-old virgin coed. I was

dressed in red, white, and blue.[36]

Even though Sebold tells her story first-person, it's striking how often circumstances required her to be intensely *looked at* and to confront herself from that same external viewpoint. Only some hours after the assault she is required by the police to be photographed. Later, in the days after the rape, she notices 'an elegant lattice work of bruises' on her body and makes out, as she puts it, 'the individual pressure points of his fingertips on my throat—a butterfly of the rapist's two thumbs interlocking in the center and his fingers fluttering out and around my neck'.[37] Frequently, recurrently, she imagines herself as seen in other people's eyes.

All of these experiences occur after Sebold had had her control over her own body taken from her in a very literal way, of course. In the opening pages of the book she recalls the details of the assault:

'Nice white titties,' he said. And the words made me give them up, lobbing off each part of my body as he claimed ownership— the mouth, the tongue, the breasts.[38]

Sebold details several methods in the months that followed by which she attempts to regain control over her body: concerted attempts to have sex with fellow students; months of dieting and exercise in an effort to lose weight. Perhaps most strikingly of all, she turns her own body into a text when she faces Madison in court:

My mother had always taught us to be scrupulous when wearing a skirt by smoothing it out before sitting down. I did this and as I did, I thought of what lay beneath the skirt and slip, still visible, if I lifted up the hem, through the flesh-tone stockings. That morning, while I dressed, I had written a note to myself on my skin. 'You will die' was inked into my legs in dark blue ballpoint. And I didn't mean me.[39]

By any measure Sebold showed phenomenal resilience and self-control in coping with what had been done to her by Madison, and in continuing to cope with the further trauma of encountering his gaze again in court (indeed a court bailiff later describes her as 'the best rape witness ever seen on the stand' in New York State). But, recalling and writing these experiences, Sebold also gestures to the sense in which she was often dissociated from herself — displaced again from her own control — by being regarded from an external viewpoint. Consider, for example, the slip in phrasing between 'I had written a note *to myself*' and the address to Madison ('"You will die" ...I didn't mean me'). The strain on the language highlights the uncomfortable way in which Sebold sought to act of her own volition while, nevertheless, occupying another person's gaze rather than her own.

This forced dissociation is perhaps most acutely exemplified when she recalls the moment in Madison's trial when she was shown the photographs which had been taken of her by the police in the hours immediately after the rape.

'I am showing you the photographs marked for identification thirteen, fourteen, fifteen, sixteen. Look at those, please.'
He handed me the photos. I looked only briefly at them.
'Are you familiar with the person depicted in those photographs?'
'Yes, I am,' I said. I placed them on the edge of the stand, away from me.
'Who is tha—?'
'Me,' I interrupted him. I began to cry. By trying not to, I made it worse.[40]

Years after *Lucky* was published, Sebold told the *Independent* how encountering the photos again while researching the memoir had affected her: 'It was intense to see the palpable absence of myself in the photos straight afterwards and that I had already taken on an intense level of shame.'[41] Similar, perhaps, to the moment in *The Comedy of Errors* when Dr Pinch, 'with no face, as 'twere, outfacing' Antipholus of Ephesus, Sebold is forcibly estranged from herself: a mirror image which doesn't show her herself but rather a 'palpable absence'.

In their article for *The Atlantic* Lukianoff and Haidt recommended that universities should 'officially and strongly discourage trigger warnings', agreeing with the opinion expressed by the American Association of University Professors in 2014: 'The presumption that students need to be protected rather than challenged in a classroom is at once infantilizing and anti-intellectual.'[42] Applying these principles to discussions of sexual assault shows very starkly what's at stake in choosing to withdraw personal agency from individual students. When I first wrote in the *Guardian* about my reasons for appending warnings to my lecture, I said that they didn't constitute censorship, but rather functioned as a basic courtesy. That courtesy is important when discussing instances of personal agency being forcibly removed from assault victims, and especially so when discussing instances with people who may potentially be assault victims themselves. The *challenge* presented to students in such cases otherwise can hardly be said to have pedagogical merit: I find it hard to understand how the courtesy of introducing a discussion properly is 'infantilizing and anti-intellectual'. One of Lukianoff and Haidt's arguments is that exposing such students to the circumstances of their trauma — seeing them 'challenged' in this way — can be therapeutic; I believe on practical grounds that this is a faulty argument, something which I'll show in the next chapter. But as we've seen in this chapter already, the principle of denying a trauma victim the individuality of their experience, of writing other people in such a way that they are formulated as a composite of external features, is a stylistic and formal hallmark of writing them in a way which is itself coercive.

Chapter 5

Thaw

When I wake up, the optician is holding me up on the seat and she looks understandably worried. Of the many eye tests she conducts every day, I would guess that comparatively few result in someone losing consciousness, and this unexpected turn of events has rattled her somewhat. For my part, I feel a great deal better: the onset of a fainting episode is horrible, an unpleasant kedgeree of hearing gone muffled and squidgy, of vision mottled purple, of movements turned heavy and far away; of impending embarrassment; of losing one's self-control. Should I ask to leave? Am I able to leave? Oh dear, too late: down I go. But look at this interlude another way: perhaps someone comes into the optician's office and sees her spread-eagled across my prone and heavy body. If she gets up to go and get help I fall to the floor, so we're stuck there in the hushed and half-lit examination room. This, surely, looks ridiculous; this, surely, is funny?

And: no harm done. The NHS website is very reassuring on this point: 'fainting (syncope) is caused by a *temporary* reduction in blood flow to the brain'.[1] In fact it's remarkably keen to stress in its short entry on the subject that fainting involves no lasting damage: 'fainting is most commonly caused by a *temporary* glitch in the autonomic nervous system'; 'an external trigger can *temporarily* cause the autonomic nervous system to stop working properly, resulting in a fall in blood pressure and fainting'; 'the trigger may also cause your heartbeat to slow down or pause for a few seconds, resulting in a *temporary* interruption to the brain's blood supply'. As horrible as the onset might feel, I suppose there's a strong case here to say I can't really whinge about it: the temporariness of this fainting state means that people often dismiss it — even ridicule it — as a weakness of constitution.

When the *Daily Mail* reported on audience members fainting during the Globe's 2014 revival of Lucy Bailey's *Titus Andronicus*, several online readers duly made fun of the 'droppers': 'NM' observed: 'Hope these losers aren't around if I have an accident and need help – pathetic'; 'Oh come on,' someone called 'Moomin' lamented, 'it's fiction not real life for goodness sake!'; 'people fainted? lol,' said 'Murty': 'pathetic'. 'Magaluf', from Leeds, put it very succinctly: 'Wimps.'[2] Press reports in general concurred with the general sense that each instance of fainting indicated weakness. Hannah Furness mused in the *Telegraph*: 'Titus Andronicus has never been one for the fainthearted'; Charles Spencer opened his review by observing: 'this is not a play for the faint-hearted'.[3] Bailey's original production in 2006 had been framed in very similar terms: the *Evening Standard* told how 'theatre-goers today warned the faint-hearted to steer clear of the Globe Theatre's gory new production of Shakespeare's bloodiest play' and Stephanie Condron's piece for the *Telegraph* was baldly headlined 'Not for the fainthearted'.[4] In these accounts, temporarily losing control of one's body by passing out is to be 'faint-hearted': 'wanting energy, courage, or will to carry a thing through; timid, cowardly', according to the *Oxford English Dictionary*.

Even if only temporary, and even though it causes no lasting harm, fainting isn't very enjoyable. Though primarily reassuring the reader that fainting is only a temporary state of affairs, the NHS website highlights one of the most unnerving aspects of the experience: in the moment of it glitching, 'the autonomic nervous system' both goes wrong *and* announces itself to us in rude terms as something separate from our conscious control. That lack of control invites us to wonder about the precise nature of the weakness alleged of the Globe 'droppers': certainly it's hard to see how a glitching autonomous nervous system has any immediate connection to 'energy, courage, or will'. Not only that, it reminds us that experiencing a lack of personal control might be very stressful in itself. Most coverage of audience members fainting in performances of *Titus Andronicus* ascribed the fainting to the play's content: 'Gore causes 100 to faint during Globe's Titus Andronicus', said the *Times*, with the *Independent* agreeing that many left 'after being overcome by on-stage gore', and the *Daily Mail* blaming 'a particularly gory five-minute scene'.[5] The scene in question seems to have been Act 2 Scene 4, when Lavinia appears on stage for the first time following her rape and mutilation. First-hand accounts from some of those physically affected by the presentation of this scene made mention of the gore, but they also stressed a particular quality of engagement with the events depicted:

> Georgina Hope, 28, an actress from London, was wiping away tears. 'I felt sick most of the time. It was the gore and the commitment of the performers. You feel part of it, they really get you involved[.]'[6]

Nicolas Bausson, a 23-year-old student, had never fainted in a performance before. Quoted in the *Independent* afterwards, he admitted: 'I'm not really comfortable with blood,' but went on to reflect that 'to imagine what had happened to her [Lavinia]... It's very disturbing.' The director, Lucy Bailey, found it 'rather wonderful' that 'people can connect so much to the characters and emotion that they have such a visceral effect'.[7] Bailey's take on Lavinia's re-entry to the stage stresses how acute that connection can be, her description notably resembling Nicolas Bausson's: 'It's hugely about her imagined pain and the shock of it all.' Lavinia's shocking appearance on stage is only part of what causes the spectators' distress: it's also their involvement with her situation which has driven them to tears, nausea and, in some cases, unconsciousness.

Knowing that my lecture on *Blasted* and *Titus Andronicus* would be discussing sexual assault fairly extensively, I was conscious that there might be people present who had experienced such assault, and who might — as a result — be suffering from post-traumatic stress disorder. Go back to the NHS website and you'll find that this isn't a condition that is termed 'temporary'; rather its symptoms 'are often severe and persistent enough to have a significant impact on the person's day-to-day life'. One of the best-known symptoms of PTSD is the reliving of the traumatic event. For an extended period following her involvement in a car crash, Siri Hustvedt was regularly woken by reliving the moment of the collision:

> the speeding van, the deafening noise of glass and metal exploding around me. For four nights in a row, I relived the shock of that van as it slammed into the passenger side of the car, where I was sitting. These were not like any memories I have ever had. I had not sought them, and they had not been triggered by some external stimulus—a smell or taste or sight or sound. They just came, and when they came, they were not in the past but in the present. The thing that had happened, happened again.[8]

In the months following her assault Alice Sebold would wake up in cold sweats believing straightforwardly that 'the rapist was inside the house': her breath 'would grow shallow', and she would promise herself that she 'would do anything the man wanted'. It's obvious from such accounts that PTSD is a condition far more severe than fainting: the only thing I can discern as common to episodes of fainting and episodes of such traumatised reliving, perhaps, is the involuntary aspects underpinning both. Hustvedt tells us that each time she woke up she did so 'sitting up in bed, terrified, my heart racing'; Sebold's breath grew shallow, she would 'feel' her door opening, feel 'a sense of another presence in the room'.[9] These are experienced as bodily afflictions: not the same as the autonomous nervous system glitching, perhaps, but in a similar way the body's steering wheel is experienced moving independent of the conscious self's grip.

Affirming that a given production will affect audience members in a physical way has become something of a trope in plays' advertising. Prominent in the coverage of the hundreds fainting during productions of Lucy Bailey's *Titus*, the Globe's spokesperson showed very little compunction about the confrontational aspects of the staging, saying 'this production is a bloody, exhilarating, incense-laden feast for the senses. But not one for the squeamish.'[10] In some quarters Bailey herself was quoted as saying: 'I used to get disappointed if only three people passed out.'[11] In crude terms, previews like this invoke this degree of physical affect as testament to how much a production immerses the spectator in what they see. When media outlets reported on my lecture having a warning attached, the founder and artistic director of the Cambridge Shakespeare Festival, David Crilly, was widely quoted lamenting the 'degree of sensitivity' on show: 'In Shakespeare,' he said, 'most of the sexual violence is implied rather than overtly stated, and whoever directs the play is responsible for how visual that is.'[12] Crilly's own 2015 production of *Titus Andronicus* was trailed in the local press as 'the Tarantino of Shakespeare plays', and while Crilly didn't like to 'give away any secrets' about the company's methods for portraying the 'gruesome aspects of the production', he did remark that he'd made sure to find a venue 'with a wooden stage – one that can be mopped clean again after every performance'.[13] Those buying tickets for this *Titus* encountered, yes, a warning:

> Please note! In keeping with Shakespeare's play our production of Titus Andronicus includes scenes of sexual violence and mutilation. Some audience members may be upset by the scenes and parental guidance is strongly advised.[14]

Previews of the play celebrated the prospect of spectators being physically affected by what they witnessed: 'this heart-pounding production is not for the faint-hearted', theatregoers were told when buying tickets online.[15] 'Faint-hearted' appears again — but it's the repetition of 'heart' ('heart-pounding'...'faint-hearted') which unconsciously emphasises how the spectator will be placed in a closed empathic loop, the spectator's heart (hopefully not too weak) will be *pounding* in concert with the hearts of the play's participants.

The facility of theatrical performance to act upon the audience in the here and now is widely recognised, and — as I've hinted here — it tends to be widely celebrated, too. When A. N. Wilson fulminated against trigger warnings in the *Daily Mail* he outlined how he thought drama could be challenging — even, in its way, torturous — *and* productive:

> At one of the most dreadful moments of King Lear, in which we have watched untold horror, a son tells his father who has had his eyes gouged out: 'Men must endure their going hence, even as their coming hither.' If we can not 'endure' reading or studying such works, how can we be expected to endure the very real tragedies which afflict our world — and to do so with the dignity of those we most admire?[16]

We might think again of Sarah Kane musing that the media outrage which welcomed *Blasted* 'was due to the play being experiential rather than speculative. The title refers not only to the content but also the impact it seems to have had on audiences. What makes the play experiential is its form.'[17] It's tempting to draw a link between the elements of theatre celebrated here — its capacities to *involve*, to *immerse* — and different forms of therapy: to this end, it's striking how some of the arguments made against my lecture's trigger warnings insisted that exposure to triggers is actively *helpful* for trauma victims.

Throughout their 2015 *Atlantic* article, Greg Lukianoff and Jonathan Haidt repeated one point in particular. A lecturer who provides trigger warnings to students 'prepares them poorly for professional life', the article argues; such provisions teach those students 'to nurture a kind of hypersensitivity that will lead them into countless drawn-out conflicts in college and beyond', it goes on. 'What are we doing to our students', Lukianoff and Haidt ask the reader, 'if we encourage them to develop extra-thin skin in the years just before they leave the cocoon of adult protection and enter the workforce?'[18] But in affirming that students should 'be taught how to live in a world full of potential offenses', Lukianoff and Haidt's *Atlantic* article wasn't just celebrating the pedagogical benefits of the university of life and the school of hard knocks; it also sought (it claimed) to safeguard students' mental wellbeing when they left their apparently coddled life on campus and emerged into the 'real world'. It argued that trigger warnings chip away at a person's powers of resilience. In their later book they cited several studies on peanut allergy to argue that point more fully: regular exposure to a source of harm, they argued, helps us develop our capacity to deal with it. This, presumably, is why they affirmed so strongly in their *Atlantic* article: 'Universities should officially and strongly discourage trigger warnings,' seeming to agree wholeheartedly with the report on trigger warnings issued by the Association of American University Professors in 2014.

Post-traumatic stress disorders differ from peanut allergies in a number of ways: too many, really, to list here, and too many, it seems, to have been acknowledged in *The Coddling of the American Mind*. But by analogising the two, Lukianoff and Haidt were trying to explain the principles underlying CBT. They tell their readers how:

Cognitive behavioral therapists treat trauma patients by exposing them to the things they find upsetting (at first in small ways, such as imagining them or looking at pictures), activating their fear, and helping them habituate (grow accustomed) to the stimuli.[19]

Trigger warnings, they argue, prevent that exposure; this, they say, is to the detriment of the student who is afflicted with PTSD, just as (by their analogy) protecting someone from their allergens doesn't address an underlying allergy. But there are some turns of phrase here which concede, implicitly, that a full lecture theatre is a terrible venue in which to conduct CBTy. The activity of a therapist does not necessarily map on to the activity of the lecturer: in lecturing on Sarah Kane my priority was not to address the victims of sexual assault who may be present in a manner 'helping them habituate ...to the stimuli'. On a strictly practical note, then, it's important to note that there's a significant difference between ignoring the possible effects of your actions upon other people and actively seeking to help other people 'to habituate' to a given stimuli. Simply claiming that the former is in fact the latter is of very limited pedagogical or therapeutic use.

Lukianoff and Haidt are correct to note how performances or lectures might resemble exposure therapy: as the psychologists Mary Beth Williams and Soili Poijula note, during sessions of direct exposure therapy the description of a traumatic event 'is done in the present tense and in great detail ...The motto behind doing this work is "no pain, no gain."' But most psychologists would also agree with the accompanying disclaimer:

Direct exposure therapy needs a great deal of preparation in order for you, as the client, to endure the process without experiencing overwhelming anxiety, suicidal thoughts, or intense fear... However, the extent of pain that can be caused by exposure therapy or overexposure to the traumatic event is too great to include it as part of the work in this workbook.

This description of exposure therapy is included here strictly as information about another way to process what has happened to you.[20]

Lukianoff and Haidt cite another psychologist, Richard McNally, who observes that 'trigger warnings are counter-therapeutic because they encourage avoidance of reminders of trauma'; however, he too seems to acknowledge that lectures have the potential to cause hurt to a student:

Severe emotional reactions triggered by course material are a signal that students need to prioritize their mental health and obtain evidence-based, cognitive-behavioral therapies that will help them overcome PTSD.

'These therapies', he says, 'involve gradual, systematic exposure to traumatic memories until their capacity to trigger distress diminishes.'[21] A lecture on Sarah Kane and William Shakespeare delivered as part of an English Faculty's provision for a third-year exam on Tragedy might well discuss traumatic material, and it might even go some way to analysing how trauma is represented, perhaps even how trauma *works* — but it's unlikely to be structured in order to provide 'gradual, systematic exposure' to any one person's traumatic memories. It's not surprising that Williams and Poijula caution that exposure therapy 'needs to be done under the guidance of a professional in a course of anywhere from nine to fourteen sessions of sixty to ninety minutes each'.[22] Even the American Association of University Professors observed, while arguing that trigger warnings were an inadequate response to PTSD, that 'the classroom is not the appropriate venue to treat PTSD, which is a medical condition that requires serious medical treatment' — an observation that Lukianoff and Haidt neglected to note in either their 2015 *Atlantic* article or their 2018 book.[23] Insofar as cognitive behavioural or direct exposure therapies might be required (or recommended) for particular students in a lecture theatre, it seems absolutely clear that it is not the place of a lecturer to believe that they're conducting that therapy when they lecture on a potentially traumatising subject. A lecturer who breaks off between PowerPoint slides to shove surprise Snickers bars into your mouth isn't helping you overcome your peanut allergy.

It's true that likening PTSD to a peanut allergy may be helpful for underscoring how inadequate and ill-suited terms like 'upset' and 'offended' are when applied to people who are suffering from PTSD and who might be at risk of a post-traumatic episode. It would be as absurd to accuse someone in anaphylactic shock of being 'faint-hearted' as it would have been to tell Siri Hustvedt to pull herself together while she 'relived the shock of that van as it slammed into the passenger side of the car'. While theatre's capacity to transport its spectators in a comparable way is often celebrated ('an incense-laden feast for the senses'!), dramatic art can also call a spectator's attention to the fact that it is being performed to them or perhaps even *at* them: asking not just 'what is happening?' but 'who is doing it — to whom, and how?' If we consider another form of therapy suggested for people with PTSD, 'Rewind' therapy, it's striking that survivors are invited to imagine themselves in a theatre of sorts: watching themselves watching a screening of 'the traumatic event as [they] experienced it or as [they] remember it in [their] dreams, flashbacks, or nightmares'.[24] Though this sounds similar to the kind of exposure which Lukianoff and Haidt propose for lecture theatres, the scenario which is described in Rewind therapy makes a point of transferring agency wholly to the survivor-spectator:

When you start the film, begin it at the point just prior to the traumatic event, seeing yourself as you were before it occurred. Remember, you are sitting in the movie theater to watch the film, but you are also in the projection room watching yourself in the theater as you watch the film. Play the film at its normal speed. Stop the film when you realized you were going to survive or when your memory begins to fade.[25]

The tantalising resemblance between this posited therapeutic space and more literal theatre spaces may well invite us to think about how movies, live drama and even lectures could foster a productive relationship between a survivor and the depiction of traumatic subject matter, helping them negotiate between the felt, inhabited experience of their trauma and a helpful critical detachment. But simply noting the broad, architectural similarities between these spaces is grossly reductive. Without taking into account the crucial sense in which a performer or a lecturer must work to grant the survivor-spectator a strong feeling of personal agency, trying to masquerade a literal theatre-space as a form of therapy is not just useless but potentially harmful.

In their book, Lukianoff and Haidt radically condense the principles of exposure and cognitive behavioural therapies: an appendix of four pages, for instance, is used to introduce the reader to the practice of CBT. In so condensing these principles they garble them, prescribing CBT as an appropriate catch-all therapy in all circumstances for all people with any mental health condition. In their version of CBT the 'patient' has no individual story — indeed, in a lecture theatre, they are not permitted an individual story, and are treated as one figure interchangeable with every single one of the people sat around them. In this parodic therapy session, the 'patient' does no talking, in fact: in Lukianoff and Haidt's preferred model for lecturing on traumatic material, the patient dutifully takes notes while the self-appointed therapist declaims from behind a lectern. As academics, Lukianoff, Haidt and I may champion the usefulness of critical detachment and the associated analytical skills enabled by it: in acknowledging that I am not a trained therapist, though, I doubt whether that academic detachment is necessarily always the same as the kinds of reflection that might help process psychiatric trauma. Though the bailiff's telling Alice Sebold that she was 'the best rape witness ever seen on the stand' may have the ring of a compliment, it may be worth pausing to think about what such a judgement entails, and what being a 'good' witness requires of the victim: forcing Sebold, in this case, to be detached from herself.[26]

As we've seen, when it was reported that trigger warnings had been appended to some Cambridge lectures this generated a great many online comments which crudely took issue with the students' critical skills: 'Did the nasty fictional play upset you?' The presentation of traumatic material in general can immerse a spectator in such a way that they 're-live' a traumatic incident, fictional or not — but we should also be attentive to the specific regard in which the *form* of that presentation (whether obviously fictional or not) may rob the spectator of their agency. In *Lucky*'s first chapter Sebold recalls the 'moment [she] signed [herself] over to' the rapist. 'I was convinced that I would not live,' she says. 'I could not fight any more. He was going to do what he wanted to me. That was it.'[27] Over the next pages she recounts the assault in painstaking detail, until she eventually describes Madison permitting her to leave.

> 'Can I go now?' I asked.
> 'Come here,' he said. 'Kiss me good-bye.' It was a date to him. For me it was happening all over again.
> I kissed him. Did I say I had free will? Do you still believe in that?[28]

The stakes are high: consolidating a survivor's sense of their own freedom as they access and analyse traumatic material would seem to be the humane thing to do, and it inconveniences no one. And in sum, it's not just humane but — practically speaking — it's helpful, too. After the initial round of media reports about the warnings appended to the lectures, I asked students who attended subsequent lectures and seminars if they wanted to share their responses: of those who got in touch to say they had benefited from such warnings, it was notable that all told me that the warnings had been used to ready themselves for the discussion to come. Far from constituting censorship, these warnings seem to have enabled more students to participate in the lectures more fully — and, importantly, on their own terms.

In this book I've used drama to try and think through how we choose to present victims of trauma. There are a few reasons for this. First, and most important to acknowledge, I'm someone who stands outside the experiences which I've seen depicted in these works and which I've then chosen to analyse in this book. I haven't been sexually assaulted; I have so far been lucky enough not to have experienced anything that I'd consider psychologically traumatic. Perhaps it's because I occupy this point of ignorance that I've found myself particularly struck by theatrical instances where victims of trauma are presented as starkly alien, inscrutable bodies — as when Sarah Kane's Cate *'laughs and laughs and laughs until she isn't laughing any more, she's crying her heart out'* before collapsing and lying still, or when Shakespeare's Lavinia is made to stand bleeding for 44 lines of someone else's monologue. These are moments, it seems to me, where dramatists are challenging their spectators to try and reach some point of empathy *despite* the difficulties encountered when perceiving the body before them to be a body unlike theirs.

The previous chapters have also shown that thinking about how 'slapstick' performance in particular, how it is manufactured and recognised as such, serves to draw our attention to the enactment of a certain set of power dynamics in action. A slapstick body is dumped on the floor, subjected to violence, emptied out of volition, all by a contriving hand and all for the entertainment of the spectator. In this light, presenting a rape victim as a slapstick body might not immerse the spectator in the spectacle so much as draw their attention to the patterns of coercion which govern it. Lavinia's eventual death underscores this: Titus, talking to the emperor, raises the case of Virginius, the centurion who killed his daughter 'with his own right hand/Because she was enforced, stained, and deflowered'. He asks Saturninus whether it was 'well done', and once Saturninus replies in the affirmative, Titus stabs his own daughter accordingly:

> A pattern, precedent, and lively warrant
> For me, most wretched, to perform the like.
> —Die, die, Lavinia, and thy shame with thee,
> And with thy shame thy father's sorrow die! **(5.3.37-8; 43-6)**

Here, as throughout the rest of the play, Lavinia has been obliged to kowtow to the aesthetic demands of others. Her singular trauma is absorbed into an artistic precedent, and her volition (already injured by Demetrius and Chiron) is finally taken from her absolutely: she is killed, *and* her identity is rendered interchangeable with Virginius's long-dead 'enforced, stained, and deflowered' daughter. Lavinia's body is used as a prop, but also as a site for abstract analysis, comparison and discussion.

By looking at more or less slapstick presentations of sexual assault in drama, my lecture tried to explore the methods by which different playwrights present the bodies of assault victims as resistant but ultimately subject to the whims of other characters and, indeed, to the playwright's own whims. In an ethically questionable way, my lectures were enacting a similar process: transforming the singular experience of being assaulted into a site of abstract discussion; indeed using the examples of assault victims as vehicles for a larger literary-critical argument. In its way this book reaffirms those problems. We have seen how Alice Sebold tried to take back possession of herself by writing a threat on her body: in some senses, an academic argument like this one takes the pen from her and writes 'READ ME' on her body, insisting that she's not so much a person as a mesh of abstract and interesting concepts, a textual item to be analysed. Even this analogy is a demonstration of what I'm talking about: re-employing another person as a figure to be exhibited, analysed, deconstructed. As we've seen in previous chapters, when slapstick modes of presentation require that we scrutinise the body of another, we note not just how it is *used* but also how it continues to possess its own inherent qualities of independence which are trampled over in that act of use. The squeamishness inspired by my analogy, in other words, arises because it demonstrably appropriates the actual body of another.

There are many other social structures of oppression and control; there are many other techniques by which people enjoying powerful positions might act out control over those in comparatively less powerful positions. But when I first started compiling the literary material for my lectures, I found it was in theatrical treatments of sexual assault in particular that the various features of 'slapstick' performance were most acutely bound up with statements of power, control and the appropriation of one person's agency by another's. In general I was willing to consider these different plays as meditations on abuse as much as they were manifestations of it: even if Sarah Kane is 'repeatedly firing a gun into the audience' in the staging of *Blasted*, I thought, its acutely confrontational and occasionally incomprehensible form invites us to wonder at it, and to attend to the power dynamics which are enacted on stage and upon us, the spectators. A lot of these same techniques are encountered in what's written about 'snowflakes', I've found, but more often than not these pieces are not meditations on power but straightforward demonstrations of it.

As we've seen, when James Delingpole gave a talk to the Cambridge University Conservative Association and many people walked out, he complained across two columns — one for *The Spectator* and one for Breitbart — about the behaviour of someone he termed a 'cry bully'. He began the column for Breitbart like this:

Reeeeeeeeeeee!
Truly it's horrible and unnerving to fall victim to a point and shriek assault by an hysterical, vengeful, feminist Social Justice Warrior.[29]

Delingpole's interpretation of events had it, then, that *he* was the victim of an assault. He seems to have been particularly upset that later that evening, when sat in a pub, he was asked to leave by a barman on the grounds that he'd said something offensive to someone on the premises. Delingpole objects that this is inaccurate — his rape jokes were conducted in the Old Parlour at Trinity College, not in the pub — and he believes the complaints to have come from two women in particular, who he has seen in the pub and recognised as two of those to have walked out of his talk. His argumentative sleight of hand is notable — '*I* was the victim, not *them!*' he implies — and it's underpinned by a careful attempt to empty his appointed adversaries of feeling (even the *capacity* to feel), presenting them instead as figures who conduct performances, devoid of any individual inner life.

The Breitbart column's curious first line — 'Reeeeeeeeeeee!' — links to a Youtube video which shows the final sequence in the 1978 remake of *Invasion of the Body Snatchers*. Here, at the film's crescendo, Brooke Adams's character Elizabeth shouts out and waves to Matthew, played by Donald Sutherland. Both have been fleeing a race of 'pod people', alien beings who create and inhabit facsimiles of humans. As Sutherland opens his mouth he emits a horrible, alien noise — which was achieved, according to various sources, by playing the sounds of pigs squealing backwards. This moment reveals dramatically that Matthew's body has been snatched too: this is not a human, merely a hitherto convincing alien simulation. The analogy seems to have floated around the internet for a period before Delingpole slapped it into his Breitbart column: in most contexts its appeal lies in its suggestion of covert invasion. '@toxicketchup' wonders in a 2014 tweet: 'I wonder if SJW's ['social justice warriors'] are just normal rational people infected with weird alien brain parasites...', for instance, adding the hashtag '#BodySnatchers'. In many other cases it's posited that 'SJWs' are *taking over*. Whatever it is snatching people's bodies is presumably meant to stand for something akin to the forces identified in right-wing paranoid fantasies of the deep state, as '@rednek_scholar' speculates:

> SJW bodysnatchers have penetrated Hollywood, Western govts, college administrations, the video game industry, and a shit ton more

In Delingpole's Breitbart column, though, one of the analogy's more local effects is to affirm that the women he upset were not human but humanoid. The transposition is undertaken in a jokey fashion, but its implications are obviously outright oppressive to the woman he re-describes, dismissing her subjective experience as a superficial performance only.

One of Delingpole's priorities, then, was to hollow those women out of any authentic, emotional existence. It's notable that even when he compares these women unfavourably with 'the most successful, brilliant, well-adjusted women' in his acquaintance, he places his reader carefully at a physical remove from the observed woman:

> They tolerate our boisterousness, our bad jokes, even our

clumsy passes because they recognise that while men have their flaws, our many countervailing virtues generally make the hassle more than worthwhile.

In this description, the brilliant, well-adjusted women who are subjected to *'our* boisterousness, *our* bad jokes… *our* clumsy passes' don't think 'this is sexual harassment' — for example — because, from this point of view, they do not think. There's an obvious power-play enacted by turning people into avatars like this. But Delingpole's domination over his described subjects is made all the more pronounced by his insistence that they occupy bodies which put up futile shows of independence and resistance. On Breitbart and in *The Spectator* the female students don't just leave or simply complain; they are variously 'hissing', in a 'frenzy', pointing and shrieking. When celebrating his cohort of successful, brilliant, well-adjusted female friends, Delingpole says they 'recognise that as intelligent, independent women they've got many, many more important things to do than perpetually look to take offence like blushing perma-victims'. Once again he dismisses his subject's ability to germinate authentic feeling (they 'look to take offence'), but once again he also acknowledges that subject's place in a body which stands before him somewhat independent of his control. Why tell us he sees it 'blushing' other than to emphasise again that the 'perma-victim' must be imagined with a physical existence — not wholly abstract, then, but subject to how he chooses to frame them?

Though I've analysed them as individual case studies, by drawing a line between Lukianoff and Haidt's thoughts on 'vindictive protectiveness' and Delingpole's complaints about the women he upset, I've tried to sketch out how these writers — and writers like them — are choosing to show trauma victims not just as figures undeserving of our sympathy but actually *incapable* of it. This book's focus on a particular set of literary techniques has shown how much cross-pollination has occurred

between academic discourses like Lukianoff and Haidt's —
which claim to attack 'vindictive protectiveness' — opinion
articles which decry 'snowflake culture', and straightforward
online hate speech. As Moira Weigel pointed out when reviewing
The Coddling of the American Mind for the *Guardian*, Haidt's
work was cited approvingly in an article for Breitbart written
by Milo Yiannopoulos and Allum Bokhuri, 'An Establishment
Conservative's Guide to the Alt-Right', while the book's recurrent
praise of Nassim Taleb's work *Antifragile* chimes with similar
enthusiasm for Taleb's work among 'the far right "manosphere"
that gathers on Reddit/pol and returnofkings.com'.[30] As we've
seen, scrolling through the comments below Delingpole's article
for Breitbart leads us to 'Mustapha Mond' and 'John' wishing rape
upon the woman singled out in the column. Delingpole seems to
have stopped replying to comments by this stage, so we can't say
he's endorsing these sentiments; nor would it be fair, necessarily,
to say he intentionally encouraged such responses in the way he
wrote the column. In the same way, it might not be fair to blame
particular writers for what seems a very widespread culture of
callousness, even vindictiveness, among such comment threads
— and, in any case, we let every individual writer off the hook if
we hold only professional writers responsible for their writing.
'Mustapha Mond' and 'John' *chose* to write what they wrote and
how they wrote it. They *choose* whether to write about other
people in a way that allows them their humanity or deprives
them of it: just as I do, and just as you do.

What, then, of the writer named in this book's title — how is
Shakespeare choosing to present victims of trauma? We might
conclude that his Lavinia functions as a criticism of the artistic
tendency to exploit female bodies and to turn them into props,
or — at best — symbols. Or maybe this is too forgiving: maybe
Lavinia is a straightforward contribution to such a tradition, a
simple avatar of yet another 'enforced, stained, and deflowered'
woman who has been over-invested with our firm belief in

Shakespeare's subtlety, complexity and overall genius. This book has held up for scrutiny several other examples where Shakespeare frames an actor's body as an alien thing — a body resembling yours or mine in several regards, but troublingly, disconcertingly strange and uncontrolled in its behaviour. I've also pointed out how other writers have done something similar for their own different ends: Kane, Delingpole, Lukianoff and Haidt and many others. But one respect in which Shakespeare comes across as a more skilful writer than any of them is how he doesn't just use the traumatised, slapstick body as a challenge to our reading: he tends to circle that body with other struggling readers. We might think of Horatio, trying to understand Hamlet ('these are wild and whirling words, my lord'); or we might think of Marcus (to Lavinia, 'Why dost not speak to me?'; to Titus, 'Why dost thou laugh?'). We might think of the onlookers berated by Lear as he presents them with the limp body of his daughter: 'Oh, you are men of stones!' (5.3.231).

In such cases the confrontational aspect of the inscrutable body may be mitigated by the sight of other people who are struggling to make sense of it. Perhaps by these means Shakespeare reformulates the *challenge* of understanding such bodies as an opportunity: allowing the audience a kind of experiential freedom of movement whereby they can identify with the baffled onlooker *and* try to identify with the afflicted body (and, perhaps, succeed in doing so). And equally, in identifying with the traumatised body and its circumstances, the spectator has then the opportunity to disengage again in order to try and process those circumstances. Compare these instances with *Blasted*, where Sarah Kane offers a much starker challenge to the spectator: demanding that they identify with a rapist or with a rape victim, or that they admit their inability to understand either figure. Or compare these with Delingpole presenting a given 'cry bully' or a given 'perma-victim' in such a way that we are supposed to stand squarely and only in his shoes, perceiving this other figure as he perceives it. As well as drawing our attention to the practice of being a spectator, by exhibiting a strange slapstick figure *and* its several interpreters on stage, Shakespeare stresses how variegated the interpretations of a slapstick figure can be; how various the experiences that inform those interpretations. As a result, we — spectators too — better realise how we and the people around us, all of us watching on together, have each of us our own distinct experiences, and so our own distinct interpretations of the traumatised body, and our own responses to it. Like the other writers considered in this book, Shakespeare presents a trauma victim as an alien figure, but unlike, say, Delingpole, he doesn't seek to meld those watching into a unanimous, adversarial entity. Delingpole and writers like him (and unlike Shakespeare) locate spectatorship in a single body of onlookers which not only stands distinct and wholly apart from that othered figure, but in single-minded opposition to it.

Part of Shakespeare's achievement in the vignettes considered in this book, then, lies in his exploration of the many possible standpoints and interpretations which crowd about the slapstick figure: a bodily text which, as we have seen, eludes any simple exposition or explanation. But when we examine how Shakespeare himself is read by — and manipulated by — some of the other writers in this book, it's notable that his knack for offering such multiple possible interpretations and such multiple possible points of empathy is suppressed. A copy of Milo Yiannopoulos's *Dangerous*, 'the most controversial book of the decade', tells its reader that 'the liberal media machine did everything they could to keep this book out of your hands' — alluding, perhaps, to his failed attempt to sue Simon & Schuster when they refused to publish it.[31] Because of that court case, a full draft of *Dangerous* marked up with editorial suggestions and known instead as 'Exhibit B' (index number 654668/2017) is now freely available to anyone who wants to read it on the New York State Courts' website (despite the very best efforts of the liberal media machine, it seems).[32] On page 56 of that manuscript Yiannopoulos, 'glad', he says, that he 'studied Shakespeare at high school', applies a ream of Shakespearean insults to Twitter's 'Black Lives Matter-loving, sandal-wearing, hobo-chic CEO Jack Dorsey':

> That trunk of humours, that bolting-hutch of beastliness, that swollen parcel of dropsies, that huge bombard of sack, that stuffed cloak-bag of guts, that roasted Manningtree ox with pudding in his belly, that reverend vice, that grey Iniquity, that father ruffian, that vanity in years.[33]

Odd, perhaps, to call a forty-something a 'grey iniquity'; and, as bombards of sack go, Dorsey doesn't appear especially huge (one website, 'allstarbio.com', claims he weighs 75 kilos). As Yiannopoulos goes on to say that 'it's fitting that the quote I chose was from *All's Well That Ends Well*, because all is indeed ending well' the quotation seems even odder; as his increasingly exasperated editor points out in the margin, the quotation is taken not from *All's Well That Ends Well* but *Henry IV Part 1*. For Yiannopoulos, the content of what he refers to is interesting, and its context isn't: attending to who speaks these lines, and why they are spoken (or even the play in which they are said) is, for Yiannopoulos, to get hung up on footling details.

Something similar is going on when Greg Lukianoff and Jonathan Haidt frame a chapter called 'The Untruth of Emotional Reasoning' with a quotation from the ancient Greek philosopher Epictetus; it's placed at the beginning of the chapter and restated in the first of several concluding bullet points delivered 'In Sum':

> What really frightens and dismays us is not external events themselves but the way in which we think about them. It

is not things that disturb us, but our interpretation of their significance.

The gist of this, they say, can be counted 'among the most universal psychological insights in the world's wisdom traditions':

> We could just as easily have quoted Buddha ('Our life is the creation of our mind') or Shakespeare ('There is nothing either good or bad, but thinking makes it so') or Milton ('The mind is its own place, and in itself can make a heaven of hell, a hell of heaven').[34]

It's helpful, perhaps, to point out that the line from Milton is spoken by Satan, and that the line from Shakespeare is given to Hamlet when he insists that 'Denmark's a prison' (2.2.231.5) — and it's necessary to wonder about the curious decision to sell the chapter's central thesis by citing endorsements from the Father of Evil and a famously unstable Danish prince.[35] Noting how radically these quotations are decontextualised begs the question again: what exactly is Shakespeare being used for? If his name is deployed here as a signal of intellectual authority, as it seems to be in Yiannopoulos's draft, then coupled with A. N. Wilson's injunction that we should '"endure" reading or studying such works' we begin to see the demands these writers are making. It's not so much a demand that we should *endure* Shakespeare, or lectures about Shakespeare, or discussions of trauma — it's a demand that the so-called snowflakes of the world should endure these writers saying whatever they think Shakespeare is saying. Whatever their merits as psychologists, therapists, sociologists (or whatever they may claim to be), by focussing on how Yiannopoulos writes, Delingpole, Lukianoff and Haidt, 'Mustapha Mond' or 'John', we need to note the acute lack of empathic skill which arises from their being chronically insensitive readers. When they imagine a figure on a stage of any sort, all are equally disinclined to attend to that figure's context; all are equally incapable of noting and analysing the forces that press in upon it as it occupies its place on that stage and in our gaze.

Michael Gove is falling over: down he goes. Shall we let him feel anything? Look at him carefully as he's falling. He's a ventriloquist's dummy — no, he's a spermatozoon in a suit! — no, it's *slime* he's made of! His legs betray him and he's on the floor. He's human, though — isn't he? — like you and me? Someone shouts that he should break his neck — another person shouts this; more join in. Do you know what he's feeling — do you *want* to?

We're watching *Titus Andronicus* at the Globe. A woman walks onto the stage: she is covered in blood; she has no hands; she has no tongue. Someone in front of us falls to the floor. Do we laugh? Staff members shoulder their way through the crowd so they can help the person who fell to the floor. Their actions are perfunctory, practised routine. The person is sitting up now. Can we laugh? They're ok. They look ok. Are they ok?

You're giving a lecture; you're reading a poem; you're performing a play; you're giving a talk. A woman rises from her seat and leaves the room. She looks upset — 'visibly distraught', in fact. But: she is leaving in the middle of your lecture — your poem — your play — your talk! Does she know how *rude* that is? How *offended* you are? 'It's ok', some voices at your shoulder tell you, 'she isn't real.' Put her in a 'muslim area', says one, 'and see how long she lasts!' Someone else says 'she'll see reality when your migrant guests give her the high hard one in the back door'. Laughter. What a funny idea.

The Winter's Tale. Act 5, Scene 3. Leontes looks upon the form of the wife he remembers; the wife he lost 16 years previously. This 'statue… but newly fixed' is extraordinarily lifelike (5.3.47). 'Would you not deem it breathed?', Leontes asks, 'and that those veins/Did verily bear blood?' (64-5) His childhood friend, Polixenes, stands next to him: 'the very life seems warm upon her lip', he observes (66). No longer *it* now but *her*, Leontes looks on: 'the fixure of her eye has motion in't', he notes, and he tells all those present

> methinks
> There is an air comes from her. What fine chisel
> Could ever yet cut breath? **(5.3.67; 77-9)**

We are all looking at Hermione as she's stood before us, just as we were all looking at her in Act One, Scene Two, when Leontes believed her to be 'slippery', 'sluiced in's absence', 'a hobby-horse' — when he told us she was an adulteress, pregnant with the child of Polixenes (273; 193; 276). In Act One Scene Two we watched her talking with Polixenes and Leontes told us they were 'paddling palms and pinching fingers', 'making practised smiles/As in a looking glass' (115-7); later, he told us, they had been 'leaning cheek to cheek... meeting noses... Kissing with inside lip' (285-6). Leontes was wrong to suspect his wife: the gods themselves revealed 'Hermione is chaste, Polixenes blameless', and 'Leontes a jealous tyrant' — but by then it was too late, Hermione was dying, shamed in front of the watching court (3.2.130-1).

'Music, awake her, strike!' Hermione's lady, Paulina, manages the spectacle, telling the lookers-on where to stand, to wait, to watch and not to touch. Music plays, and the figure before us moves. Leontes is instructed to present his hand to her. She takes it: he says 'O, she's warm!' (109). This was never a statue, of course: Shakespeare's somehow tricked us into acknowledging what we can see quite clearly in front of us. This so-called statue was always just a human body: warm, breathing, motion in its eye, animated by a magic 'lawful as eating' (111). Those who were estranged are reconciled, spare characters are married off.

All's well that ends well.

The play is over. That was a happy ending — wasn't it? The play's story has shown us people in pain, true, and we saw several consequences of Leontes' actions that haven't been undone: his son, Mamillius, still dead; Paulina's husband, Antigonus, still very much eaten by a bear. But that statue coming to life, the repentant onlooker reconciled with the very person he wronged — watching this makes us feel good, no? But long after we leave the theatre-space perhaps we continue to reflect on what we've seen, and perhaps we find that the spectacle is still somehow troubling. We can try and call it the magic of theatre, so we worry about it less; but didn't Shakespeare have to go to extraordinary efforts to remind us that the person we were all looking at — this whole time — is a person exactly like us?

Notes and References

Chapter 1
Snowflakes

1 Nathan Bevan, 'Tommy Cooper's last act fooled us all, says Jimmy Tarbuck', *Wales Online*, first published 12 April 2009; https://www.walesonline.co.uk/news/wales-news/tommy-coopers-last-act-fooled-2111280

2 John Fleming, '"I Was There in the Theatre That Night" — The Death of Tommy Cooper, Live on TV', *Huffington Post*, first published 28 May 2012; https://preview.tinyurl.com/y5nt535j

3 David Quantick, 'Tommy Cooper: genius or fool?', the *Telegraph*, first published 15 April 2014; https://www.telegraph.co.uk/culture/tvandradio/tv-and-radio-reviews/10768370/Tommy-Cooper-genius-or-fool.html

4 Ian MacEwan, 'David Threlfall as Tommy Cooper: "It was daunting to play the so-called funniest man in Britain"', *What's On TV*, first published 17 April 2014; Tarbuck quoted in Bevan, 'Tommy Cooper's last act'.

5 'Six famous faces celebrate Tommy Cooper', *Radio Times*, 21 April 2014; https://www.radiotimes.com/news/2014-04-21/six-famous-faces-celebrate-tommy-cooper

6 'Tommy Cooper Dies Live on Stage', posted on YouTube by 'TVQU1Z on twitter', 15 April 2018. At the time of writing the video has had 689,665 views and is still active. All comments quoted are taken from the thread below this video.

7 Chris Irvine, 'Footage of Tommy Cooper's death on stage shown on YouTube', the *Telegraph*, first published 9 May 2009; https://www.telegraph.co.uk/technology/news/5298541/Footage-of-Tommy-Coopers-death-on-stage-shown-on-YouTube.html. Davies was also quoted by Paul Revoir, 'YouTube storm over video showing Tommy Cooper's death on stage', *MailOnline*, 9 May 2009; https://www.dailymail.

co.uk/tvshowbiz/article-1179569/YouTube-storm-video-showing-Tommy-Coopers-death-stage.html

8 'The Cambridge English Course', University of Cambridge Faculty of English website, https://www.english.cam.ac.uk/admissions/undergraduate/course.htm

9 Camilla Turner, 'Cambridge students warned Shakespeare plays may distress them', the *Telegraph*, 18 October 2017; https://www.telegraph.co.uk/education/2017/10/18/cambridge-university-students-given-trigger-warning-shakespeare. BBC News, 'Cambridge Uni students get Shakespeare trigger warnings', 19 October 2017; https://www.bbc.co.uk/news/uk-england-cambridgeshire-41678937

10 Alia Shoaib, 'Cambridge University issues trigger warnings for Shakespeare lecture', *The Guardian*, 19 October 2017; https://www.theguardian.com/education/2017/oct/19/cambridge-university-issues-trigger-warnings-for-shakespeare-lecture. Eleanor Harding, 'Alas, poor snowflakes: Cambridge University issues warnings about sex and violence in Shakespeare and Greek tragedy — in case students get upset', *Mail Online*, 18 October 2017; https://www.dailymail.co.uk/news/article-4994688/Cambridge-warns-students-Shakespeare-studies.html

11 'Cambridge University slammed over Shakespeare "trigger warnings"', Fox News, 19 October 2017; https://www.fox news.com/world/cambridge-university-slammed-over-shakespeare-trigger-warnings. Tom Ciccotta, 'Cambridge University issues "trigger warnings" over Shakespeare reading', Breitbart, 20 October 2017; https://www.breitbart.com/tech/2017/10/20/cambridge-university-issues-trigger-warnings-over-shakespeare-reading

12 Except where stated otherwise all *MailOnline* comments are taken from the thread beneath Eleanor Harding, 'Alas, poor snowflakes'. 'Heatherbelle', Epsom; 'bar', Notts; 'Hactov', Yorkshire; 'Sian Carvill', Ras Al Khaimah, UAE.

13 'carolo', Henley.

14 'OLD SPARKY', Utopia Lincolnshire; 'angus mccoatup', Manchester.

15 Except where stated otherwise, all Shakespeare quotations have been taken from the third edition of *The Norton Shakespeare*, ed. Stephen Greenblatt *et al* (New York: W. W. Norton & Company, 2016). All line numbers, act and scene divisions accord with this edition.

16 Except where stated otherwise, I have taken all *Blasted* quotations from *Sarah Kane: Complete Plays* (London: Bloomsbury Methuen Drama, 2016).

17 David Mitchell, 'The trouble with getting lost in your own world...', *The Observer*, 22 October 2017; https://www.theguardian.com/commentisfree/2017/oct/22/cambridge-university-trigger-warnings-piccadilly-circus-targeted-advertising-david-mitchell. For Mitchell's later apology, see 'When life imitates the art of the sitcom', *The Observer*, 5 November 2017; https://www.theguardian.com/commentisfree/2017/nov/05/when-life-imitates-sitcom-woman-pulled-over-by-dog

18 'Sasha', Cornwall; 'aberrant_apostrophe', Reading; 'Proudoldman', London.

19 Alex Clayton, *The Body in Hollywood Slapstick* (London: McFarland & Company, Inc., 2007) pp. 173-4.

20 James Pembroke, 'Trigger Unhappy', *The Oldie*, 19 October 2017; https://www.theoldie.co.uk/blog/trigger-unhappy

21 Alan Dale, *Comedy is a Man in Trouble: Slapstick in American Movies* (Minnesota: University of Minnesota Press, 2000) p. 12.

22 Tony Staveacre, *Slapstick! The Illustrated History of Knockabout Comedy* (London: Angus & Robertson, 1987) p. 41.

23 'Free thought', Cardiff; 'Mr Babbage', Somewhere else, Switzerland.

24 'BabyOhBaby', NYC-London.

25 'Travalinman', London.

26 'angus mccoatup', Manchester.

27 A. N. Wilson, 'Cambridge students who need "trigger warnings" about sex and murder in Shakespeare may as well need Noddy', 20 October, 2017; https://www.dailymail.co.uk/news/article-4999160/A-N-WILSON-Cambridge-sex-murder-Shakespeare.html

28 Jack Tinker, 'This Disgusting Feast of Filth', *Daily Mail*, 19 January 1995.

29 Quentin Letts, 'Blasted: Cannibalism and nudity. The Loony Left will love it!', *MailOnline*, 4 November 2010; https://www.dailymail.co.uk/tvshowbiz/reviews/article-1326742/Blasted-Cannibalism-nudity-The-Loony-Left-love-it.html

30 Quentin Letts, 'Cliched prison play is torture for all concerned: QUENTIN LETTS' first night review of Cleansed by Sarah Kane', *MailOnline*, 24 February 2016; https://www.dailymail.co.uk/tvshowbiz/article-3461342/Cliched-prison-play-torture-concerned-QUENTIN-LETTS-night-review-Cleansed-Sarah-Kane.html

31 *Johnson on Shakespeare*, vols VII and VIII ed. Arthur Sherbo (New Haven: Yale University Press, 1968) in *The Yale Edition of the Works of Samuel Johnson* (multiple vols, 1955-2010); vol VIII p. 704.

32 'The Tragedies of Shakespeare': originally published in *The Reflector* IV (1811); taken here from *Charles Lamb on Shakespeare*, ed. Joan Coldwell (Colin Smythe: Gerrards Cross, 1978) pp. 24-42, p. 36.

33 James Delingpole, 'Delingpole World', delingpoleworld.com/about-james-delingpole; Milo Yiannopoulos, *Dangerous*, 'About the Author' — see, for instance, https://www.amazon.co.uk/Dangerous-Milo-Yiannopoulos/dp/069289344X; Greg Lukianoff and Jonathan Haidt, *The Coddling of the American Mind*, (London: Allen Lane, 2018), back inside flap hardback edition.

34 Quoted in Aleks Sierz, *In-yer-face Theatre: British Drama*

Today (London: Faber and Faber, 2001) p. 97.

35 Diogenes Laertius, *Lives of Eminent Philosophers* trans. R. D. Hicks (Cambridge, Massachusetts: Harvard University Press, 1980), 2 vols, vol I, p. 327.

36 *Oxford English Dictionary*, 'snowflake, n.', 'Draft additions January 2018'; https://www.oed.com/view/Entry/183512

Chapter 2
Falling Down

1 Christopher Marlowe, *Doctor Faustus*, in *Christopher Marlowe: The Complete Plays* ed. Frank Romany and Robert Lindsey (London: Penguin, 2003); epilogue, ll. 4-6.

2 John Milton, *Paradise Lost* in *John Milton: The Major Works* ed. Stephen Orgel and Jonathan Goldberg (Oxford: Oxford University Press, 2003), I.76. All further references to *Paradise Lost* are taken from this edition.

3 Aristotle *Poetics,* trans. and ed. Malcolm Heath (London: Penguin, 1996) pp. 20-1.

4 *The Body in Hollywood Slapstick*, p. 13.

5 Henri Bergson, 'Laughter', first published in French 1900; taken in English from *Comedy* ed. Wylie Sypher (Baltimore: Johns Hopkins University Press, 1986), pp. 61-190, p. 78.

6 Simon Shepherd, *Theatre, Body and Pleasure* (London: Routledge, 2006) p. 46.

7 Ravelhofer and Caroso quoted in Shepherd, p. 46.

8 'Michael Gove falls over', video posted on YouTube by 'jaotheraccount2', 11 July 2010; https://www.youtube.com/watch?v=HAqyf7a4xFM. All YouTube comments are taken from the thread below this video except where stated otherwise.

9 *The Body in Hollywood Slapstick*, pp. 173-4.

10 'Ben Willock'.

11 Plutarch, 'The Life of Antonius', in *Selected Lives from the Lives of the Noble Grecians and Romans* trans. James Amyot

and subsequently Thomas North, ed. Paul Turner (Fontwell: Centaur Press Limited, 1963) 2 vols, vol II; pp. 104-61, p. 106.

12 T. S. Eliot, 'Shakespeare and the Stoicism of Seneca', in *Selected Essays* (London: Faber and Faber, 1999) pp. 126-40, pp. 130-1.

13 For more on the *pietà* motif, see Margreta de Grazia, *'King Lear* in BC Albion', in *Medieval Shakespeare* ed. Ruth Morse, Helen Cooper and Peter Holland (Cambridge: Cambridge University Press, 2013), pp. 138-56. The resemblance between the *pietà* and the 'image of that horror' in *Lear* has been noted frequently: de Grazia cites several studies which comment on the link, such as Robert Hunter, *King Lear: The John Coffin Memorial Lecture, 1966* (London: Athlone Press, 1967); Helen Gardner *King Lear: The John Coffin Memorial Lecture, 1966* (London: Athlone Press, 1967); C. L. Barber, 'On Christianity and the Family: Tragedy of the Sacred', in *Twentieth Century Interpretations of 'King Lear'* ed. Janet Adelman (Englewood Cliffs, NJ: Prentice-Hall, 1978), pp. 117-9; Helen Cooper, 'Shakespeare and the Mystery Plays', in *Shakespeare and Elizabethan Popular Culture* ed. Stuart Gillespie and Neil Rhodes (London: Thomson Learning, 2006), pp. 18-41; and Katherine Goodland, *Female Mourning in Medieval and Renaissance English Drama* (Aldershot: Ashgate, 2005). de Grazia's chapter is also illustrated with various examples of the *pietà* current in Shakespeare's time and in the centuries preceding: a fifteenth century English sculpture now held by the Musée de Cluny in Paris, a woodcut taken from Thomas à Kempis, *A Treatyse of ye Imitation of Cryst* (London: Richard Pynson, 1503/4), a stained-glass window at the Church of St Peter and St Paul at East Harling, in Norfolk, and a wall painting at Thame Parish Church in Oxfordshire.

14 'The Tragedies of Shakespeare', p. 36.

Chapter 3
Slosh

1 'First custard pie thrown on film', *Guinness Book of World Records* website; www.guinnessworldrecords.com/world-records/first-custard-pie-thrown-on-film

2 Louise Peacock, *Slapstick and Comic Performance: Comedy and Pain* (Basingstoke: Palgrave Macmillan, 2014) p. 23.

3 *Comedy is a Man in Trouble*, p. 12.

4 *Slapstick and Comic Performance*, p. 22.

5 Millie Taylor, *British Pantomime Performance* (Bristol: Intellect Books, 2007) p. 35.

6 These words from W. C. Fields are widely quoted: I have taken them here from Tony Staveacre, *Slapstick!*, p. 10. Staveacre, though — like many others — omits the following (taken from Max Eastman, *Enjoyment of Laughter* (New Brunswick: Transaction Publishers, 2009; originally published Simon and Schuster, 1936) p. 336):

> I try to pretend that it isn't painful. I try to hide the pain with embarrassment, and the more I do that, the better they like it. But that doesn't mean they are unsympathetic. Oh no, they laugh often with tears in their eyes. Only of course it mustn't be *too* painful. I never would try to make love funny, for instance. I was in love once myself, and that's too painful—that's too painful!

7 Staveacre, *Slapstick!* p. 41.

8 From James Johnson's *Account of Pantomime* (London: H. S. Phillips, 1884), quoted in Edwin M. Eigner, 'Imps, Dames and Principal Boys: Gender Confusion in the Nineteenth-Century Pantomime', *Browning Institute Studies* 17 (1989) pp. 65-74, p. 69.

9 James Pembroke, 'Trigger Unhappy'.

10 Letter to Mary Elizabeth Tayler, 6 November 1849, in *The

Letters of Charles Dickens, ed. Madeline House and Graham Storey, 12 vols (Oxford: Clarendon Press, 1965-2002); Vol V, p. 640.

11 Rosalind Crone, 'Mr and Mrs Punch in Nineteenth-century England', *The Historical Journal* 49:4 (2006), pp. 1055-82; p. 1065.

12 *Slapstick and Comic Performance*, p. 70.

13 ibid, p. 20.

14 ibid, p. 27.

15 Jack Tinker, 'This Disgusting Feast of Filth', *Daily Mail*, 19 January 1995.

16 The RADA production, staged in association with Graeae, was staged between 6-16 February 2019. Those buying tickets on the RADA website (https://www.rada.ac.uk/ whats-on/blasted/) could click through to a detailed list of content warnings, which I provide in full below, and which can be accessed via the following URL: https://graeae.org/ blasted-2019-content-warnings/

Jenny Sealey's 2019 production of Blasted at RADA will not be presented as naturalistic.
However, the play is upsetting and challenging, and the following content warnings apply and our age recommendation is 16+:
Multiple references / depictions of sexual assault / rape / child abuse
Coercion
Racist language
Homophobic language
Misogynistic language
Strong violence
Deceased infant
Smoking and alcohol use
War

Descriptions of torture
References to murder
References to genocide
Bombs
Suicide
Cannibalism
Full frontal nudity

17 *Sarah Kane: Complete Plays*, p. x.
18 *In-yer-face Theatre*, p. 97.
19 *British Pantomime Performance*, p. 41.
20 *In-yer-face Theatre*, p. 100.
21 *Slapstick and Comic Performance*, p. 128.
22 *In-yer-face Theatre*, p. 103.
23 Jane Edwardes, *Time Out*, 25 January 1995 (quoted in *In-yer-face Theatre*, p. 95).
24 UK Ministry of Justice, Home Office, and Office for National Statistics, *An Overview of Sexual Offending in England and Wales*, 'Overview' p. 6; https://www.gov.uk/government/statistics/an-overview-of-sexual-offending-in-england-and-wales, published 10 January 2013.
25 *In-yer-face Theatre*, p. 98.
26 'Delingpole: My Horrible, Horrible Encounter with a "Rape Culture" Cry Bully at Cambridge University', Breitbart, 30 June 2018, https://www.breitbart.com/europe/2018/06/30/how-offended-student-lied-get-me-thrown-out-pub/; 'My encounter with the self-righteous cry-bullies of Cambridge', *The Spectator*, 30 June 2018, https://www.spectator.co.uk/2018/06/my-encounter-with-the-self-righteous-cry-bullies-of-cambridge/. All Breitbart comments which are quoted here have been taken from the thread below Delingpole's article.
27 Connor MacDonald, 'The CUCA walkout is what political correctness should look like', *Varsity*, 20 June 2018, https://

www.varsity.co.uk/opinion/15845.

28 David Mitchell, 'The trouble with getting lost in your own world...'; A. N. Wilson, 'Cambridge students who need "trigger warnings" about sex and murder in Shakespeare may as well need Noddy'.

Chapter 4
No Two Alike

1 Stefan Kanfer, *Groucho: The Life and Times of Julius Henry Marx* (London: Penguin, 2000) p. 106.

2 ibid, p. 22.

3 ibid, p. 139. It's not clear whether this was, in actuality, a fairly standard case of understudying rather than a concerted *trick*. The *Variety* review of the 8 November performance (printed 12 November 1930) seems to know exactly what's going on: 'With Groucho in the Michael Reese Hospital with appendicitis, and Zeppo wearing his mustache and clothes, the performance of the brothers lacked spirit. Zeppo was adept at the substitution and when the boys know where they stand it will be okay.' That said, the four performing brothers are said to have dressed up as each other to confusing and comic effect on numerous other occasions, and Kanfer does go on to quote Zeppo saying of this particular switcheroo that 'some of [Groucho's] friends didn't even realize it was me. But it got pretty bad after a few days, because I never smoked cigars, and I'd smoke those goddamn cigars every day. I used to vomit every day after the last show—four or five shows a day, and it was very difficult.' For whatever reason, the notion that the brothers could swap their personas easily and completely seems to have been celebrated by a significant number of people (including the brothers themselves).

4 Danny Leigh, 'The Marx Brothers on film: souped-up comedy', *Financial Times*, 2 January 2015; https://www.ft.com/content/79d9cd22-89f7-11e4-8daa-00144feabdc0

5   *Slapstick!*, p. 5.

6   *British Pantomime Performance*, p. 35.

7   ibid, p. 35.

8   Charles Spencer, 'One Man, Two Guvnors, Haymarket Theatre Royal, Review', *Telegraph*, 14 March 2012, https://www.telegr aph.co.uk/culture/theatre/theatre-reviews/9144394/One-Man-Two-Guvnors-Haymarket-Theatre-Royal-review.html; Michael Billington, 'One Man, Two Guvnors, [Lyttelton, Lon don] - Review', 25 May 2011, https://www.theguardian.com/ stage/2011/may/25/one-man-two-guvnors-review

9   Charles Spencer, 'One Man, Two Guvnors, Adelphi Theatre, review', *Telegraph*, 22 November 2011, https://www.tele graph.co.uk/culture/theatre/theatre-reviews/8905164/One-Man-Two-Guvnors-Adelphi-Theatre-review.html

10 Royal Shakespeare Company, https://www.rsc.org.uk/the-comedy-of-errors/past-productions

11 Royal Shakespeare Company, https://www.rsc.org.uk/the-comedy-of-errors/past-productions/productions-1938-2005

12 'will i am not', Cardiff, comment on 'Alas, poor snowflakes', *MailOnline*.

13 Greg Lukianoff and Jonathan Haidt, 'The Coddling of the American Mind', *The Atlantic,* September 2015, https://www. theatlantic.com/magazine/archive/2015/09/the-coddling-of-the-american-mind/399356/

14 'How America reacted to "The Coddling of the American Mind"', uploaded 14 March 2016, www.youtube.com/ watch?time_continue=3&v=BwMeZLh1C8E

15 *The Coddling of the American Mind*, (London: Allen Lane, 2018) p. 11.

16 'The Coddling of the American Mind'.

17 *Oxford English Dictionary*, 'snowflake, n.', 'Draft additions January 2018'; https://www.oed.com/view/Entry/183512

18 Praise taken from the amazon.co.uk page for *Trauma and Recovery: The Aftermath of Violence — From Domestic Abuse*

to Political Terror, 3rd edn (New York: Basic Books, 2015); remarks attributed to Gloria Steinem and the original *New York Times* review (written by Phyllis Chesler in 1992). Herman, *Trauma and Recovery* p. 51.

19 *Trauma and Recovery*, p. 56.
20 ibid, p. 1.
21 ibid, p. 73.
22 Alice Sebold, *Lucky* (London: Picador, 2002) p. 22.
23 Alice Sebold, 'HERS; Speaking of the Unspeakable', *New York Times*, 26 February 1989, https://www.nytimes.com/1989/02/26/magazine/hers-speaking-of-the-unspeakable.html
24 *Lucky*, p. 213.
25 *Coddling of the American Mind*, pp. 31-2.
26 ibid, p. 26.
27 ibid, p. 25.
28 Siri Hustvedt, *The Shaking Woman, Or, A History of My Nerves* (London: Sceptre, 2010) p 4.
29 ibid, p. 5.
30 ibid, p. 186.
31 ibid, p. 188.
32 ibid, p. 188.
33 ibid, p. 36.
34 ibid, p. 36.
35 *Lucky*, p. 39.
36 ibid, p. 180.
37 ibid, p. 28.
38 ibid, p. 16.
39 ibid, p. 181.
40 ibid, pp. 182-3.
41 Christina Patterson, 'Alice Sebold: Rape and redemption', *Independent*, 6 June 2003, https://www.independent.co.uk/arts-entertainment/books/features/alice-sebold-rape-and-redemption-107713.html
42 American Association of University Professors, 'On Trigger

Warnings', August 2014, https://www.aaup.org/report/ trigger-warnings

Chapter 5
Thaw

1   NHS website, 'Fainting — Causes'; www.nhs.uk/conditions/ fainting/causes/

2   'Audience members FAINT during bloodthirsty showing of Shakespeare's Titus Andronicus', *MailOnline*, 1 May 2014; https://www.dailymail.co.uk/news/article-2617420/Five-faint-Shakespeares-Globe-bloodiest-play-Gruesome-scene-Titus-Andronicus-brings-audience-knees.html

3   Hannah Furness, 'Globe audience faints at "grotesquely violent" Titus Andronicus', *Telegraph*, 30 April 2014, www.telegraph.co.uk/culture/theatre/william-shakespeare/10798599/Globe-audience-faints-at-grotesquely-violent-Titus-Andronicus.html; Charles Spencer, 'Titus Andronicus, review: "a dramatic power that makes the stomach churn and the hands sweat"', *Telegraph*, 2 May 2014, www.telegraph.co.uk/culture/theatre/theatre-reviews/10803436/Titus-Andronicus-review-a-dramatic-power-that-makes-the-stomach-churn-and-the-hands-sweat.html

4   Rashid Razaq, 'Globe lays on the gore', *Evening Standard*, 5 June 2006, www.standard.co.uk/go/london/theatre/globe-lays-on-the-gore-7299012.html; Stephanie Condron, 'Not for the fainthearted', *Telegraph*, 3 June 2006, www.telegraph.co.uk/news/uknews/1520196/Not-for-the-fainthearted.html

5   Jack Malvern, 'Gore causes 100 to faint during Globe's Titus Andronicus', *The Times*, 24 July 2014, www.thetimes.co.uk/article/gore-causes-100-to-faint-during-globes-titus-andronicus-bdqrmdgvwf8; Nick Clark, 'Globe Theatre takes out 100 audience members with its gory Titus Andronicus', *Independent*, 22 July 2014, www.independent.co.uk/arts-entertainment/theatre-dance/news/globe-

theatre-takes-out-100-audience-members-with-its-gory-titus-andronicus-9621763.html; 'Audience members FAINT during bloodthirsty showing of Shakespeare's Titus Andronicus', *MailOnline*, 1 May 2014, www.dailymail.co.uk/news/article-2617420/Five-faint-Shakespeares-Globe-bloodiest-play-Gruesome-scene-Titus-Andronicus-brings-audience-knees.html

6   Quoted in Oscar Quine, 'Got the stomach for Titus Andronicus?', *Independent*, 2 May 2014, www.independent.co.uk/arts-entertainment/theatre-dance/news/got-the-stomach-for-titus-andronicus-9318962.html

7   Quoted in Nick Clark, 'Globe Theatre takes out 100 audience members...', *Independent*

8   *The Shaking Woman*, p. 43.

9   *Lucky*, pp. 236-7.

10 This statement was widely quoted: see, for instance, Furness, 'Globe audience faints at "grotesquely violent" Titus Andronicus', *Telegraph*, and 'Audience members FAINT...', *MailOnline*.

11 Quoted in Nick Clark, 'Globe Theatre takes out 100 audience members...', *Independent*.

12 Crilly was quoted in almost all of the initial coverage of the lecture's warning. See Camilla Turner, 'Cambridge students warned Shakespeare plays may distress them', *Telegraph*; Eleanor Harding, 'Alas, poor snowflakes', *MailOnline*; Alia Shoaib, 'Cambridge University issues trigger warnings for Shakespeare lectures', *Guardian*. Crilly's opinions about 'academic freedom' made it across the Atlantic: he featured in the *Washington Examiner* (Tom Rogan, 'Cambridge University embraces safe space idiocy', 19 October 2017); on Fox News ('Cambridge University slammed over Shakespeare "trigger warnings"', 19 October 2017); and on Breitbart (Tom Ciccotta, 'Cambridge University issues "trigger warnings" over Shakespeare reading', 20 October 2017).

13 'What's on at Cambridge Shakespeare Festival', *Cambridge Edition*, 6 July 2015, cambsedition.co.uk/?arts-culture=whats-on-cambridge-shakespeare-festival; Jenny Shelton, 'Cambridge Shakespeare Festival 2015', *Cambridge Edition*, 6 July 2015.

14 Cambridge Live Tickets, 'Cambridge Shakespeare Festival – Titus Andronicus', https://www.cambridgelive.org.uk/ticke ts/events/cambridge-shakespeare-festival-titus-andronicus

15 https://www.cambridgelive.org.uk/tickets/events/cam bridge-shakespeare-festival-titus-andronicus

16 A. N. Wilson, 'Cambridge students who need "trigger warnings" about sex and murder in Shakespeare may as well need Noddy'.

17 *In-yer-face Theatre*, p. 98.

18 Coddling of the American Mind.

19 *Coddling of the American Mind*, p. 29.

20 Mary Beth Williams and Soili Poijula, *The PTSD Workbook* 3rd edn (Oakland, California: New Harbinger, 2016), p. 88.

21 Quoted in *Coddling of the American Mind*, p. 29.

22 *PTSD Workbook*, p. 88.

23 American Association of University Professors, 'On Trigger Warnings', August 2014, https://www.aaup.org/report/trig ger-warnings

24 *PTSD Workbook*, p. 65.

25 ibid, p. 65.

26 *Lucky*, p. 206. This remark has been seized upon and widely quoted in profiles of Sebold: see Christina Patterson, 'Alice Sebold — Rape and redemption', *Independent*; Katharine Viner, 'Above and beyond', *Guardian*, 24 August 2002, www.theguardian.com/books/2002/aug/24/fiction.features; 'I share my life with my rapist', *The Scotsman*, 8 June 2003, www.scotsman.com/arts-and-culture/books/i-share-my-life-with-my-rapist-1-1290478; Robert McCrum, 'Adventures in Disturbia', *Guardian*, 14 October 2007, www.theguardian.

com/books/2007/oct/14/fiction.features; 'Profile: Alice Sebold', the *Times*, 29 November 2009, www.thetimes.co.uk/article/ profile-alice-sebold-x53wmn65msp

27 *Lucky*, p. 14.

28 ibid, p. 21.

29 'Delingpole: My Horrible, Horrible Encounter with a "Rape Culture" Cry Bully at Cambridge University'.

30 Moira Weigel 'The Coddling of the American Mind review — how elite US liberals turned rightwards', *Guardian*, 20 September 2018, https://www.theguardian.com/books/2018/ sep/20/the-coddling-of-the-american-mind-review

31 Taken from the amazon.co.uk page for Milo Yiannopoulos, *Dangerous* (Dangerous Books, 2017).

32 'Exhibit B', New York State Courts' website, *Milo Yiannopoulos vs Simon & Schuster*, case number 654668 (2017); https:// iapps.courts.state.ny.us/fbem/DocumentDisplayServlet?do cumentId=VhVQNjyOxzgx32b52YsZJg==&system=prod

33 ibid, p. 56.

34 *Coddling of the American Mind*, pp. 33; 50; 34.

35 It might be contended that Satan is at this point urging the legions of hell to make the best of a decidedly bad situation ('Better to reign in hell, than serve in heaven', he tells them (1.263)). But even if Lukianoff and Haidt are intent on commending Satan's positive mindset, we should note that his positivity is very short-lived. Consider a little later, for example:

> Me miserable! which way shall I fly
> Infinite wrath and infinite despair?
> Which way I fly is hell; myself am hell;
> And in the lowest deep a lower deep
> Still threatening to devour me opens wide,
> To which the hell I suffer seems a heaven. (4.73-8)

It's unclear whether Lukianoff and Haidt believe that Satan's experience of Hell is a cognitive distortion. This would constitute a highly unusual reading of *Paradise Lost*; weighing up its merits is, unfortunately, beyond the remit of this study.

CULTURE, SOCIETY & POLITICS

The modern world is at an impasse. Disasters scroll across our smartphone screens and we're invited to like, follow or upvote, but critical thinking is harder and harder to find. Rather than connecting us in common struggle and debate, the internet has sped up and deepened a long-standing process of alienation and atomization. Zer0 Books wants to work against this trend. With critical theory as our jumping off point, we aim to publish books that make our readers uncomfortable. We want to move beyond received opinions.

Zer0 Books is on the left and wants to reinvent the left. We are sick of the injustice, the suffering, and the stupidity that defines both our political and cultural world, and we aim to find a new foundation for a new struggle.

If this book has helped you to clarify an idea, solve a problem or extend your knowledge, you may want to check out our online content as well. Look for Zer0 Books: Advancing Conversations in the iTunes directory and for our Zer0 Books YouTube channel.

Popular videos include:

Žižek and the Double Blackmain

The Intellectual Dark Web is a Bad Sign

Can there be an Anti-SJW Left?

Answering Jordan Peterson on Marxism

Follow us on Facebook
at https://www.facebook.com/ZeroBooks and Twitter at https://
twitter.com/Zer0Books

Bestsellers from Zer0 Books include:

Give Them An Argument
Logic for the Left
Ben Burgis
Many serious leftists have learned to distrust talk of logic. This is
a serious mistake.
Paperback: 978-1-78904-210-8 ebook: 978-1-78904-211-5

Poor but Sexy
Culture Clashes in Europe East and West
Agata Pyzik
How the East stayed East and the West stayed West.
Paperback: 978-1-78099-394-2 ebook: 978-1-78099-395-9

An Anthropology of Nothing in Particular
Martin Demant Frederiksen
A journey into the social lives of meaninglessness.
Paperback: 978-1-78535-699-5 ebook: 978-1-78535-700-8

In the Dust of This Planet
Horror of Philosophy vol. 1
Eugene Thacker
In the first of a series of three books on the Horror of Philosophy,
In the Dust of This Planet offers the genre of horror as a way of
thinking about the unthinkable.
Paperback: 978-1-84694-676-9 ebook: 978-1-78099-010-1

The End of Oulipo?
An Attempt to Exhaust a Movement
Lauren Elkin, Veronica Esposito
Paperback: 978-1-78099-655-4 ebook: 978-1-78099-656-1

Capitalist Realism
Is There no Alternative?
Mark Fisher
An analysis of the ways in which capitalism has presented itself
as the only realistic political-economic system.
Paperback: 978-1-84694-317-1 ebook: 978-1-78099-734-6

Rebel Rebel
Chris O'Leary
David Bowie: every single song. Everything you want to know,
everything you didn't know.
Paperback: 978-1-78099-244-0 ebook: 978-1-78099-713-1

Kill All Normies
Angela Nagle
Online culture wars from 4chan and Tumblr to Trump.
Paperback: 978-1- 78535-543-1 ebook: 978-1-78535-544-8

Cartographies of the Absolute
Alberto Toscano, Jeff Kinkle
An aesthetics of the economy for the twenty-first century.
Paperback: 978-1-78099-275-4 ebook: 978-1-78279-973-3

Malign Velocities
Accelerationism and Capitalism
Benjamin Noys
Long listed for the Bread and Roses Prize 2015, *Malign Velocities*
argues against the need for speed, tracking acceleration
as the symptom of the ongoing crises of capitalism.
Paperback: 978-1-78279-300-7 ebook: 978-1-78279-299-4

Meat Market
Female Flesh under Capitalism
Laurie Penny
A feminist dissection of women's bodies as the fleshy fulcrum of
capitalist cannibalism, whereby women are both consumers and
consumed.
Paperback: 978-1-84694-521-2 ebook: 978-1-84694-782-7

Babbling Corpse
Vaporwave and the Commodification of Ghosts
Grafton Tanner
Paperback: 978-1-78279-759-3 ebook: 978-1-78279-760-9

New Work New Culture
Work we want and a culture that strengthens us
Frithjoff Bergmann
A serious alternative for mankind and the planet.
Paperback: 978-1-78904-064-7 ebook: 978-1-78904-065-4

Romeo and Juliet in Palestine
Teaching Under Occupation
Tom Sperlinger
Life in the West Bank, the nature of pedagogy and the role of a
university under occupation.
Paperback: 978-1-78279-637-4 ebook: 978-1-78279-636-7

Ghosts of My Life
Writings on Depression, Hauntology and Lost Futures
Mark Fisher
Paperback: 978-1-78099-226-6 ebook: 978-1-78279-624-4

Sweetening the Pill
or How We Got Hooked on Hormonal Birth Control
Holly Grigg-Spall
Has contraception liberated or oppressed women?
Sweetening the Pill breaks the silence on the dark side of hormonal
contraception.
Paperback: 978-1-78099-607-3 ebook: 978-1-78099-608-0

Why Are We The Good Guys?
Reclaiming your Mind from the Delusions of Propaganda
David Cromwell
A provocative challenge to the standard ideology that Western
power is a benevolent force in the world.
Paperback: 978-1-78099-365-2 ebook: 978-1-78099-366-9

The Writing on the Wall
On the Decomposition of Capitalism and its Critics
Anselm Jappe, Alastair Hemmens
A new approach to the meaning of social emancipation.
Paperback: 978-1-78535-581-3 ebook: 978-1-78535-582-0

Enjoying It
Candy Crush and Capitalism
Alfie Bown
A study of enjoyment and of the enjoyment of studying. Bown asks what enjoyment says about us and what we say about enjoyment, and why.
Paperback: 978-1-78535-155-6 ebook: 978-1-78535-156-3

Color, Facture, Art and Design
Iona Singh
This materialist definition of fine-art develops guidelines for architecture, design, cultural-studies and ultimately social change.
Paperback: 978-1-78099-629-5 ebook: 978-1-78099-630-1

Neglected or Misunderstood
The Radical Feminism of Shulamith Firestone
Victoria Margree
An interrogation of issues surrounding gender, biology, sexuality, work and technology, and the ways in which our imaginations continue to be in thrall to ideologies of maternity and the nuclear family.
Paperback: 978-1-78535-539-4 ebook: 978-1-78535-540-0

How to Dismantle the NHS in 10 Easy Steps (Second Edition)
Youssef El-Gingihy
The story of how your NHS was sold off and why you will have to buy private health insurance soon. A new expanded second edition with chapters on junior doctors' strikes and government blueprints for US-style healthcare.
Paperback: 978-1-78904-178-1 ebook: 978-1-78904-179-8

Digesting Recipes
The Art of Culinary Notation
Susannah Worth
A recipe is an instruction, the imperative tone of the expert, but this constraint can offer its own kind of potential. A recipe need not be a domestic trap but might instead offer escape – something to fantasise about or aspire to.
Paperback: 978-1-78279-860-6 ebook: 978-1-78279-859-0